# A Guide to Information Sources for Social Work and the Human Services

by Henry Neil Mendelsohn

Phoenix ● New York

ORYX PRESS

1987

The rare Arabian Oryx is believed to have inspired the myth of the unicorn. This desert antelope became virtually extinct in the early 1960s. At that time several groups of international conservationists arranged to have 9 animals sent to the Phoenix Zoo to be the nucleus of a captive breeding herd. Today the Oryx population is over 500, and herds have been returned to reserves in Israel, Jordan, and Oman.

Copyright © 1987 by
The Oryx Press
2214 N. Central at Encanto
Phoenix, AZ 85004-1483

Published simultaneously in Canada

Printed and Bound in the United States of America

∞ The paper used in this publication meets the minimum requirements of American National Standard for Information Science—Permanence of Paper for Printed Library Materials, ANSI Z39.48, 1984.

**Library of Congress Cataloging-in-Publication Data**

Mendelsohn, Henry N.
  A guide to information sources for social work and the human services.

  Includes bibliographies and index.
  1. Social service—Library resources—United States.
  2. Social service—United States—Bibliography.
  3. Reference Books—Social service.  I. Title.
  HV91.M43  1987        026'.36        87-12253
  ISBN 0-89774-338-5

# CONTENTS

# INTRODUCTION

Social work is becoming increasingly empirical and is developing a considerable body of organized literature. In addition, those who work in the field use the literatures of related academic disciplines, such as psychology, psychiatry, sociology and public administration.

Because the literatures of social work and the related disciplines are growing rapidly, it is difficult to quickly locate needed information. The purpose of this book is to systematically present pertinent sources that social work practitioners, educators and students can use to locate information in libraries.

This guide is organized around the assumption that library research is probably going to be utilized to write term papers or reports, or as part of a research project. It is my belief that library research should be conducted in a systematic organized manner, and the particular approach I advocate is reflected in the way the book is organized.

Chapter 1 provides an overview of how libraries are organized and the services they provide. Chapter 2 describes informational sources such as directories, dictionaries and encyclopedias that provide brief information. Also included are handbooks. Handbooks, like encyclopedias, present topical overviews and may provide bibliographies.

Chapter 3 describes indexing and abstracting services that can be used to find journal and newspaper articles. Chapter 4 provides an overview of social work and related journals and describes 100 such journals. Chapter 5 describes computerized literature searches and numerous relevant databases.

Chapter 6 addresses the role of books in the literature search and how to locate them. Chapter 7 discusses the use of public documents and how they can be acquired. Chapter 8 summarizes use of statistical data in social work and social welfare and how to locate statistical information.

Because social workers are often legally bound by rules and regulations they must follow in providing services and frequently involved in the policymaking process, it is important to know how to find out about the law. Legal sources, as well as a brief overview of the legal system, are presented in Chapter 9. Chapter 10 describes how to find historical and archival information. Finally, Chapter 11 gives suggestions for keeping up with new literature.

Each chapter includes definitions of the sources as well as an explanation of where they fit in the social science literature. The sources are grouped by subject rather than by format. Thus, even though Chapter 3 discusses social science indexes and abstracts, other indexes are described in additional chapters. For example, indexes to statistical reports are in Chapter 8, "Statistics," and indexes to history journals are in Chapter 10, "Historical Information." There is some repetition of sources where necessary, but I have tried to keep such repetition to a minimum.

Sources are presented in narrative form with complete bibliographic citations at the end of each chapter. Many of the source annotations are descriptive, but when possible I have tried to be evaluative and to steer researchers toward the best sources. This guide is selective; guides to other subjects are mentioned where appropriate. Many other subject guides can be located in most large libraries or by consulting a reference librarian.

This guide culminates several years of work in learning and writing about the bibliographic aspects of social work and social welfare. I believe it fills a gap in the literature, and I hope it will be useful for social workers and social work educators.

I would welcome reader comments and suggestions for future editions.

*Henry Neil Mendelsohn*
*Bibliographer and Reference Librarian for Social*
*  Work and Criminal Justice*
*Graduate Library for Public Affairs and Policy*
*State University of New York at Albany*

# CHAPTER 1
# How Libraries Are Organized

Understanding how libraries are organized aids the process of exploiting the richness of the materials contained within them. Large libraries are complex, bureaucratic institutions that collect, organize, store and make publicly available the knowledge and culture of a society. Libraries collect not only books and journals but also information contained in other formats, such as phonograph records, photographs, videotapes, films, computer disks, data tapes, microfilm, and microfiche.

Libraries vary greatly in size, resources, purpose and abilities. They range in size from the small public library in a back room of a local municipal building to the all-encompassing Library of Congress. Many libraries are general in nature; that is, they collect materials in many subject areas and try to meet a wide variety of public needs. Other libraries are specialized, devoting their efforts and resources to meet specific needs, such as medicine or law or the history and culture of a minority group.

Libraries today cannot and do not attempt to be all things to all people. Libraries have been overwhelmed by the information explosion and rapid technological changes and greatly hindered by inflation, usually coupled with declining financial support.

To help overcome these latter trends, most individual libraries have organized themselves into networks that share collections and resources. Chapter 6, "Books," mentions two national resource-sharing networks: OCLC and RLIN. Libraries join such networks to help classify and catalog their materials and to aid in the sharing of materials among libraries. For example, it is not necessary to travel to New York City or San Francisco or London to get a book from a library in one of those cities. Even the smallest of public libraries can usually arrange to obtain the needed materials through the mail.

Just as libraries differ in purpose and size, they also differ in organization. However, most libraries follow similar organizational schemes, and it is this general pattern that this chapter explains. In addition to explaining how libraries are organized, there is a discussion of the services libraries provide and the people who provide the services. Most of the emphasis is on the organization of college, university and large public libraries.

## TECHNICAL SERVICES

Large libraries are divided along functional lines. The "marking and parking" of books and other materials is carried out in the technical services departments that the public usually does not see. Technical services departments are broken down into smaller components. There is usually an acquisitions department that orders and receives the materials. Acquisitions departments often contract with commercial companies that buy books in large batches from publishers and are thus able to sell them to libraries at a discount. A library tells the commercial vendors what types of materials in which subjects they want, and the vendors attempt to match the library's needs. It saves acquisitions librarians from having to individually order every book and journal at full price. Not all materials can be obtained this way. Librarians still must spend a great deal of time directly ordering individual items from publishers.

Once the books and other materials are received, they are sent to the cataloging department, where they are cataloged and classified, i.e., assigned subject headings and call numbers and have catalog cards produced for them. The large bibliographic utilities (OCLC and RLIN), more fully explained in Chapter 6, aid in this process.

There are units within technical services departments that maintain the card catalog or online catalog, bind and mend the materials, and accept and process gifts. Librarians generally head or manage the various units, and because many library processes are now automated, library technicians or assistants often perform much of the routine work.

## PUBLIC SERVICES

The shelving and circulation of materials, reference and research services, and some aspects of collection development (buying the books) are considered public services. Books and other materials are organized according to a classification scheme so that they can usually be quickly found. Both the Dewey Decimal and Library of Congress classification schemes are briefly explained in Chapter 6. The card or online catalog, also more fully described in the same chapter, serves as a library's index to its materials and as a compendium of the knowledge contained within the materials.

## REFERENCE SERVICES

The public usually begins looking for books and other materials in the card or online catalog or in the indexes and abstracts to the journal literature. Most libraries organize their indexes in what is called the reference department. This is the area where most of the dictionaries, encyclopedias, bibliographies, almanacs, and handbooks are kept. Such materials usually cannot be taken out of the library.

Most libraries provide help in accessing their materials. The librarians who provide the help are reference librarians. They are trained in the use and interpretation of the myriad secondary sources that access the primary literature. Reference librarians will interpret the card or online catalog, steer people toward the best indexing or abstracting service for their needs, find dictionaries and encyclopedias, and assist in using other reference materials.

## SUBJECT SPECIALISTS

Many large college, university and public libraries employ reference librarians who, in addition to a graduate library degree, have second master's degrees or Ph.D.s in a subject area. Thus, an education librarian may have a master's degree in education, a science librarian may have a biology or chemistry degree, a social science librarian a sociology or anthropology degree and so forth. This trend toward specialization has occurred as society and libraries have become more specialized.

These subject specialists often buy many of the books and other materials. In addition to the books that are automatically received, materials are bought by subject specialists, also called bibliographers, to help fill in the gaps. They manage sections of the collections and in many cases help the public find and use the materials. Some librarians only buy books and some only provide reference services, but many librarians do both.

As far as the public is concerned, the reference librarian is by far the most important resource in the library. If the library you are using does not own something you need, the reference librarians can help you find which library does and help you obtain it. They can often suggest the best reference source to use to find needed information. They can interpret indexes, abstracts and library policies, such as circulation policies. Librarians in some large, urban, public libraries provide information and referral services to the public in much the same way as some social workers.

## COMPUTER SEARCH SERVICES

Information is frequently stored in computerized databases and many libraries offer access to them. This is often referred to as a computer search service.

Libraries that offer computer search services often include the service within the reference department. Because computer searches cost money and libraries have tight budgets, they often pass on to the public part or all of the costs. Smaller libraries cannot always provide computer search services but may well be able to take your request and send it to a larger library that will perform the search. For example, the New York State Library performs computer searches for New York libraries that cannot afford the service themselves.

Fortunately, many libraries can afford the service, and some even allow the public to do their own searches using equipment and instructions provided by the library. If your library does provide public access and instruction for computer searches, it is well worth your time to learn the basics of computer searching. More and more libraries are acquiring microcomputers for public use. Libraries that can afford to do so buy the computers and software and provide instruction in their use.

## CIRCULATION

Once you have found what you need you will probably want to take it home to use. Libraries vary widely in circulation policies. Private college and university libraries may let only their own students and faculty borrow materials. Or they may charge the public a borrowing fee. Most will let the public use their materials on site, but again, policies vary.

Reference books and journals usually cannot be taken out. Exceptions can be made, but you must present a good reason for wanting to be an exception. Most libraries suffer from a high degree of theft and mutilation of materials and for such reasons are not always as trusting as the public may want them to be. Books in the main part of the collection may be taken out, but time periods, fine policies, and borrowing policies vary. Most libraries serve a specific population or geographical area and restrict borrowing according to such criteria. However, as more and more libraries share resources due to declining budgets, they are setting up cooperative borrowing privileges. For example, you may be able to obtain a card from your local library that lets you check out books from another area library. It is in your best interest to find out what the options are.

## INTERLIBRARY LOAN

Another cooperative service is interlibrary loan. ILL is often a separate department or office within the library that helps you obtain needed materials from other libraries when the library you are using does not have them. Libraries are linked electronically across the country, through OCLC, RLIN and other utilities, in order to readily identify who owns what and to send materials back and forth through the mail. Most libraries are generous in what they loan but often restrict the lending of old and rare materials. For example, you may be able to obtain a rare book through ILL but be required to use it in the library, sometimes under supervision. Again, this is to prevent theft and mutilation.

## GOVERNMENT DOCUMENTS AND MAPS

Chapter 7, "Public Documents," explains how publications from the federal, state and local governments are accessed and organized. Public documents, especially federal government publications, are often housed separately from the other materials and organized according to a different classification scheme. Libraries also vary widely in what documents they collect but generally have many of the most important documents. Federal publications are disseminated widely across the country and are generally obtainable. It is important when first looking for government publications to inquire about what publications a library has and how you would go about finding them. Libraries often employ librarians who specialize in document librarianship.

Maps of all types are also usually housed separately from the books and journals. So too are materials in microform. Both require special storage and careful use, and there are often librarians who specialize in these areas who can help you.

## SPECIAL COLLECTIONS AND ARCHIVES

Many large libraries have separate areas for old and rare books. These departments are called special collections, and, again, there are librarians who specialize in this area. Libraries often collect in specific special areas, such as regional history and literature, literature from a particular period or geographical area, or literature devoted to a specific subject. Materials that are likely to be stolen or mutilated, such as art books, are also often housed in a special collections department.

Archives contain public or institutional records of historic interest, as opposed to documents of current interest. Papers of notable individuals, such as a university president or an important politician, are archival material. The records of an organization or institution are, if deemed worth keeping, kept in archives. The persons who manage archives are called archivists and may or may not also be librarians. Archival work is a narrow, but no less important, specialty.

Special collections and archives can be fascinating places worth exploring. Public use is often restricted to help preserve the materials, but interested persons only need inquire with the person in charge to gain access.

## MICROFORMS

Increasingly, more material—newspapers, documents, books, and journals—is available only in microform. The most common microforms are microfilm and microfiche. Microform is one answer to limited space, a problem in most libraries, and serves as a means to preserve older materials. Many collections of research materials, such as those mentioned in Chapter 10, "Historical Information," are available only in the library that houses them. Since they are too rare or valuable to send through the mail via interlibrary loan, they are often microfilmed. Microfilming may be done by a commercial company which then sells the films to libraries. Many valuable research collections have been widely disseminated in microform.

Many other types of materials are available in microform. Most doctoral dissertations written in the U.S. and Canada are microfilmed by University Microfilms International (UMI) and sold on demand. UMI also microfilms old and rare books, which are then printed and sold on demand.

The U.S. Government Printing Office recently embarked on a campaign to publish many documents only in microform. The U.S. Census was one such publication scheduled only for microform, but libraries and members of the public protested the sole use of microform, maintaining that it restricted access. Many libraries have been given a choice of paper copy or microform for many documents, but the trend toward microform is irreversible.

Newspapers are also frequently microfilmed. The expense of maintaining collections of newspapers in paper copy is prohibitive. Newspaper does not last long, and it is bulky. Most major newspapers are microfilmed by commercial companies and the films sold to libraries.

Although microforms are not as easy to use as paper copies, they are an important medium for preserving older materials and for widely disseminating research collections. They are also a good way to store large volumes of materials in small spaces.

## CONCLUSION

Libraries need not be difficult or confusing to use. Because libraries have to serve many different groups of people and must meet many different needs, they have evolved systematic methods of acquiring, organizing and preserving information. Libraries today are overwhelmed by the huge body of published information contained in numerous formats. They are usually underfinanced and understaffed, which can lead to confusion and disappointment on the part of library users.

Libraries are not supermarkets. They cannot always provide instant gratification and do not have numerous copies of every book and journal, unlike a supermarket, which usually has what you need when you need it. However, if used with patience and an understanding of what they can and cannot do, libraries are surprisingly good providers of information. Public support is needed in order to ensure quality public libraries.

# CHAPTER 2
# Brief Information: Reference Books

Looking for brief information, as opposed to books and journal articles, can be a time-consuming and confusing task given the plethora of reference books available in any library. A reference book arranges and treats its subject matter in a way that allows for quickly finding discrete items of information. It need not be read cover to cover but merely opened to the correct page or section in order to find what is needed.

There are as many types of reference sources as there are questions. A reference source need not be a book. Many reference sources exist as computerized databases. However, this chapter focuses on various types of printed reference books, including general sources, bibliographies, dictionaries, encyclopedias, handbooks, biographical sources and directories. Not all of the sources described in this chapter will be available in a small- to medium-sized public library. Many will only be found in college or university libraries, especially those serving a human services clientele. Your local library will help you identify which library has a particular source and provide a phone number for that library.

Before using any reference book for the first time it is wise to read the introduction or preface that describes the source in order to find out how to use it correctly and efficiently and to ascertain what it includes and excludes.

## GENERAL SOURCES

A good general source for locating other reference books is Webb's *Sources of Information in the Social Sciences: A Guide to the Literature* (1986). It defines the social sciences broadly to include general social science literature, history, geography, economic and business administration, sociology, anthropology, psychology, education and political science. An excellent introduction describes the evolution of the social sciences and their literature. Each chapter provides detailed listings of works in each specialty and subdiscipline as well as a narrative overview of the field. Social work sources are included in the chapter on sociology.

Sheehy's *Guide to Reference Books* (1986) serves as a guide to research in all major areas. Its British counterpart is *Walford's Guide to Reference Material* (1980), which provides an annotated listing of over 10,000 reference sources and is international in scope but with a strong British slant. Ryder's *Canadian Reference Sources: A Selective Guide* (1981) serves as a guide to locating Canadian literature.

## BIBLIOGRAPHIES

A bibliography is a list of works, documents and/or bibliographic items usually having some relationship among them, such as all the works by a given author, on a given subject, or published in a particular place. A bibliography is usually systematically arranged in a consistent form.

Bibliographies may be found in many places: at the end of a chapter in a book, at the end of a journal or encyclopedia article, or in book form. Generally, a bibliography or list of references will provide you with a basic bibliographic citation. If the citation is to a book, it will provide the name of the author or editor, the title of the book, where it was published and by whom, the date of publication and sometimes the number of pages. A bibliographic citation to a journal article should give you the author or authors, title of the article, the journal in which it was published, the volume and issue of the journal, the pages and usually the date of publication. Many bibliographies also provide annotations of each item describing the item and sometimes analyzing its usefulness or quality. Obviously, annotated bibliographies are the most helpful.

All the bibliographies on topics relevant to social work are too numerous to list here. But there are several useful reference works that serve as guides to locating bibliographies. Although dated, Besterman's *A World Bibliography of Bibliographies and Bibliographical Catalogues, Calendars, Abstracts, Digests, Indexes and the Like* (1966) still is a standard work. It provides an alphabetical subject arrangement of over 117,000 bibliographies with annotations.

The *Bibliographic Index: A Cumulative Bibliography of Bibliographies* is a subject listing of bibliographies published separately or appearing as parts of books, pamphlets, and periodicals. Each bibliography must have 50 or more citations to be included. This index is particularly useful for identifying bibliographies contained within larger works. It is published three times a year.

Conrad's *References Sources in Social Work: An Annotated Bibliography* (1982) pulls into one volume the major reference sources in social work as well as many allied disciplines. Each entry is described. It includes numerous citations to bibliographies on specific subjects and should be useful for social work students seeking to quickly locate a bibliography on a pertinent topic.

There are general bibliographic sources for locating books and journals. *Books in Print* is an annual cumulation listing in-print and forthcoming book titles and their prices from over 18,000 publishers. "In print" means books available for purchase from the publisher. Those that are no longer published are called out of print. *Books in Print* is divided into three parts: *Authors, Titles* and *Subject Guide*. The *Subject Guide* uses Library of Congress subject headings and might prove useful for compiling a current bibliography.

Two publications that are published more frequently than *Books in Print* are the *Cumulative Book Index,* a monthly listing of English language books (cumulations date back to 1896) and *Publisher's Weekly: The Book Industry Journal,* which provides weekly lists of new books.

Journals and other periodically published works can be located in *Ulrich's International Periodicals Directory* or *The Standard Periodical Directory.* Ulrich's is international in scope and is arranged by subject. The section entitled "Social Services and Welfare" covers social work journals. *The Standard Periodical Directory* lists over 65,000 periodicals from the U.S. and Canada by subject. Both sources provide basic ordering information and names of editors.

## DICTIONARIES

Dictionaries contain the words of a language or the terms of a subject arranged in some definite order, usually alphabetic, with explanations of their meanings, pronunciations, etymologies, and syntactical and idiomatic uses. They may either describe how words are used in everyday discourse or prescribe the proper use of words. A dictionary devoted to a particular subject often considers the meanings of terms in relation to a larger body of knowledge. It not only defines but attempts to assess the suitability of the usage. A good specialized or subject dictionary may also place words within the broader concepts of a field or within a particular school of thought or the works of a particular writer.

Social work and other social and behavioral sciences often use everyday words but assign different meanings or use them in specific contexts. When writing any type of paper, it is important to define what is meant by usage of a particular term or concept. Encyclopedias may also provide definitions of terms.

Until recently there was no American dictionary of social work. The National Association of Social Workers has filled this gap with Barker's *Dictionary of Social Work* (1987). It defines over 3,000 terms frequently used in social work.

Both Clegg's *Dictionary of Social Services, Policy and Practice* (1980) and Timms' *Dictionary of Social Welfare* (1982) define social work and social policy terms and concepts as used in Britain. Clegg also refers to British laws and acts of Parliament. Both are useful for comparative research. Mitchell's *A New Dictionary of Sociology* (1979) is also a British publication. Because social work borrows from and utilizes research and terminology from related social and behavioral sciences, this dictionary is useful for locating concise definitions of sociological terms. Fisher's *The Dictionary of Mental Health* (1980) presents numerous definitions of mental health terms and concepts with a slightly British twist. A useful American publication is the American Psychiatric Association's *A Psychiatric Glossary: The Meanings of Terms Frequently Used in Psychiatry* (1981).

## ENCYCLOPEDIAS

Encyclopedias are systematic summaries of knowledge. A universal or general encyclopedia popularizes scholarship and knowledge for a nonscholarly audience. A specialized or subject encyclopedia presents a cumulation of research results. An encyclopedia gives a broader focus than is given in the research literature, which tends to focus on limited, specific problems or questions. The broader focus provides generalizations drawn from specific research. It states what is known about a subject within a unified organizational framework. Encyclopedias pick up where dictionaries leave off. A dictionary defines while an encyclopedia not only defines but interprets and places knowledge within a larger framework.

A specialized encyclopedia is a good place to begin researching a new subject. The articles are usually written by authorities in the field and provide overviews of subjects and definitions of terms. Bibliographies are generally provided at the end of each article. There is a variety of specialized encyclopedias for social work and related fields. In addition to the ones described here, there are numerous other specialized encyclopedias for just about every subject.

The National Association of Social Worker's *Encyclopedia of Social Work* (1986) is the only encyclopedia devoted entirely to social work. First published in 1965 it supersedes the *Social Work Yearbook* (1929–1964). The *Yearbook* was a record of organized efforts to deal with social problems. The *Encyclopedia* is greatly expanded and, unlike the *Yearbook,* includes biographical information and statistical data on social problems. More information is included, reflecting a broader definition of the social sciences.

Those trends are reflected in the current 18th edition. The *Encyclopedia* claims to present materials on the entire range of activities in social welfare and social work. There are 225 articles, all of which were written expressly for the 18th edition. The subject areas of the 17th edition (1977) were revised and rewritten by "leading scholars in their field of expertise." Several new subjects were added that reflect changes in social welfare and social work in the 1980s. Among the new and expanded articles are "Computers and Information Services," "Sexual Orientation," "Women's Issues," "Political Action," "Deinstitutionalization," "Workplace," "Direct Practice," and "Volunteers." Each of the articles contains extensive references, and, because of their currentness, the articles and references are a good starting point for a topical overview and for beginning a literature search.

To help the user obtain useful articles there are 26 reader's guides that help identify related articles on a topic. For example, under the general topic of poverty and income support there are 12 articles, including "Child Support," "Income Distribution," and "Nutrition Programs." In addition, each article contains cross-references to related articles.

One major organizational change in the 18th edition was to group the biographical sketches in a separate section rather than in an alphabetic sequence with the topical articles. There are 99 biographies of persons who made outstanding contributions to social welfare and social work. Another major change was to present the statistical section in a separate, third volume. In the previous editions the statistical section was included as an appendix in the back of the second and final volume. The new separate volume contains 96 pages of data relating to social welfare. Much of it is in graphic form. The statistical tables are annotated and refer to original sources. This is an important point since the data presented may be only part of the original source. NASW says that it will offer revisions of the statistical volume during the life span of the 18th edition in order to keep it up-to-date. The two primary volumes include an extensive index; the third, statistical volume has its own index.

Complementing the *Encyclopedia of Social Work* is Romanofsky's *Social Service Organizations* (1978) which lists in alphabetical order 293 social service organizations, both current and historical, that have had a major impact on the social services. Many are national organizations, but prominent local agencies are also included. Emphasis is on historical sketches of organizations compiled from difficult to obtain primary sources. For example, the historical development of the National Association of Social Workers is traced and a bibliography of sources is included.

Kuper's *The Social Science Encyclopedia* (1985) presents over 700 entries concerned with theories, issues, methods and biographies. The major social sciences are covered in-depth. The 500 contributors are from 25 different countries, thus providing international perspectives and diversity. This encyclopedia should serve as a useful update to the *International Encyclopedia of the Social Sciences* (1968), a 17-volume set which, although dated, remains the standard work in the field and is familiar to many social scientists and students. It is, in addition to its coverage of the social sciences, a good source for psychological and social psychological information. There is considerable biographical coverage.

The field of psychiatry is thoroughly covered in Arieti's *American Handbook of Psychiatry* (1975), a six-volume set organized around foundations, child and adolescent psychiatry, sociocultural and community psychiatry, adult clinical psychiatry, organic disorders and psychosomatic medicine, treatment, and new psychiatric frontiers.

Eidelberg's *Encyclopedia of Psychoanalysis* (1968) presents lengthy definitions and articles on most psychoanalytic concepts. General concepts such as envy, jealousy and love are included as well as more specific terminology. A more recent work is Wolman's *International Encyclopedia of Psychiatry, Psychology, Psychoanalysis, and*

*Neurology* (1977), a multivolume work presenting a comprehensive overview of psychology and related fields. Approximately 2,000 contributors contributed over 1,900 articles covering both broad and narrow topics in "the various branches dealing with human nature, its deficiencies, and their treatment."

Even more recent is Corsini's *Encyclopedia of Psychology* (1984). The editor says that the articles in this encyclopedia are written not only for specialists and professionals but also for the intelligent layperson "in the argument that professionals are laypeople when not reading in their own specialized field." This work can be used for three purposes: (1) basic, quick information, such as a definition or correct spelling, (2) summary information about a particular subject or person (there are 2,100 separate entries on subjects and people), and (3) a basic text on all of psychology or as supplemental reading for shorter texts.

Woody's *Encyclopedia of Clinical Assessment* (1981) provides an overview of clinical assessment. It covers conceptual framework, individual development, major disorders, personality development, sexuality, planning and prognostic factors, etc.

Three additional encyclopedias that should be useful for social workers and students are Kruskal's *International Encyclopedia of Statistics* (1978) which presents definitions and lengthy articles on the entire field of statistics; Hegel's *Encyclopedia of Management* (1982) which covers most management concepts and terms; and Kadish's *Encyclopedia of Crime and Justice* (1983). The last work represents an interdisciplinary approach to the study of criminal behavior and the responses of society to it. Included are such broad and interdisciplinary topics as "the nature and causes of criminal behavior of various kinds, the prevention of crime, the punishment and treatment of offenders, the functioning of the institutions of criminal justice, and the bodies of law that define criminal behavior and govern the processes through which the criminal law is applied." There is a useful section entitled "Guide to Legal Literature," which includes a glossary of terms and a legal index divided into two parts, a table of cases, and a topical arrangement of legal documents. There is also a general index.

## HANDBOOKS

Handbooks are generally considered to be compendiums covering one or more subjects and of basic or advanced level, arranged for the quick location of facts and, most importantly, capable of being carried (as opposed to a multivolume encyclopedia or bulky dictionary). They may supply answers to specific questions, such as statistics, rules, or quotations. They may, in broader form, organize, summarize and make readily accessible a body of basic information about a field of study. Some of the handbooks listed here stray from this definition. They may actually be closer to texts or collections of articles on a specific field of study. Some are also multivolume works. However, they define themselves as handbooks and so are included in this section. Also included are a couple of works that are not considered handbooks but serve as such by organizing, summarizing and facilitating access to a body of knowledge about a field of study.

Handbooks are included in this section because they may serve essentially as encyclopedias by providing an overview of a subject, definitions, and extensive bibliographies. They may supplement an encyclopedia article or provide good background reading where no encyclopedia article exists. Numerous handbooks published in recent years should be useful for social workers and social work students. A selection is described here.

## Aging

The *Handbook of Aging and the Social Sciences* (1976), edited by Binstock, is arranged in five parts: (1) "Social Aspects of Aging," (2) "Aging and Social Structure," (3) "Aging and Social Systems," (4) "Aging and Interpersonal Behavior," and (5) "Aging and Social Intervention." It is part of the Handbook of Aging series published by Van Nostrand Reinhold. Also included in the series are the *Handbook of the Biology of Aging* (1977), edited by Finch; the *Handbook of the Psychology of Aging* (1985), edited by Birren; the *Handbook of Geriatric Psychiatry* (1980), edited by Busse; the *Handbook of Gerontological Services* (1985), edited by Monk; Cohen's *Funding in Aging: Public, Private and Voluntary* (1979); and Norback's *Older American's Handbook: Practical Information and Help on Medical and Nursing Care, Housing, Recreation, Legal Services, Employment, In-Home Services, Food, Associations and Organizations, Transportation and Mental Health and Counseling for Older and Retired Americans* (1979).

They are complemented by Palmore's *Handbook on the Aged in the United States* (1984) and Birren's *Handbook of Mental Health and Aging* (1980). Social services for the elderly are covered in Holmes' *Handbook of Human Services for Older Persons* (1979).

The *Sourcebook on Aging* (1979) is an excellent reference book which provides recent information on the elderly. It includes many statistical tables and charts in addition to a wealth of information on many subjects concerning the elderly. The statistical data presented in the *Sourcebook* are brought up-to-date by Schick's *Statistical Handbook on Aging Americans* (1986). Data cover demographics, social characteristics, health, employment, economic status, and expenditures for the elderly.

## Assessment

The current standard diagnostic manual for classification of mental disorders is the *Diagnostic and Statistical Manual of Mental Disorders*, 3rd edition (1980). It is commonly referred to as *DSMIII*. It was prepared over a period of years by the American Psychiatric Association. Chapters and subchapters end with lengthy bibliographies. A useful guide explaining the use of *DSMIII* is Webb's *DSMIII Training Guide for Use with the American Psychiatric Association's Diagnostic and Statistical Manual of Mental Disorders*, 3rd edition (1981). It is recommended by the APA.

Handbooks which cover the topic of assessment are Ciminero's *Handbook of Behavioral Assessment* (1977), which addresses numerous topics in behavioral assessment; the *Handbook of Psychological Assessment*, edited by Goldstein (1984), covering psychometrics and psychological tests; Groth-Marnet's *Handbook of Psychological Assessment* (1984), also covering psychological and personality tests; and Kellerman's *Handbook of Psychodiagnostic Testing: Personality Analysis and Report Writing* (1981).

## Behavior Therapy and Behavior Modification

Behavior therapy and behavior modification are widely used tools in social work and psychology. Various aspects of these topics are treated in Goldstein's and Foa's *Handbook of Behavioral Interventions: A Clinical Guide* (1980), which covers behavior therapy as does Hensen's *Handbook of Clinical Behavior Therapy with Adults* (1985). Leitenberg addresses both topics in the *Handbook of Behavior Modification and Behavior Therapy* (1976), which emphasizes the empirical evaluation of therapy techniques and outcomes using applied operant research. Behavior modification with the mentally retarded is covered in Matson's *Handbook of Behavior Modification with the Mentally Retarded* (1981). A more general text is Turner's *Handbook of Clinical*

*Behavior Therapy* (1981). Fisher's *Handbook of Behavior Therapy with Sexual Problems* (1977) focuses on sexual disorders and deviations and behavior therapy.

## Childhood and Adolescence

Osofsky's *Handbook of Infant Development* (1979) reviews current theories, data, and research findings on children from birth to two years of age. Mussen's *Handbook of Child Psychology* (1983) is a broad, four-volume set: (V1) *History, Theories and Methods*, (V2) *Infancy and Biological Bases of Development*, (V3) *Cognitive Development*, and (V4) *Socialization, Personality and Social Development*. Walker's *Handbook of Clinical Child Psychology* (1983) covers clinical approaches and child psychotherapy. Childhood psychological disorders are addressed in Ollendick's *Handbook of Child Psychopathology* (1983). Child sexual abuse is treated in Sgroi's *Handbook of Clinical Intervention in Child Sexual Abuse* (1981). Bernstein's *Handbook of Psychiatric Consultation with Children and Youth* (1984) is concerned with child psychiatry and psychiatric consultation.

Adolescence is covered in three texts: Adelson's *Handbook of Adolescent Psychology* (1980), Malmquist's *Handbook of Adolescence: Psychopathology, Antisocial Development, Psychotherapy* (1978), and Pravder's *Handbook of Adolescents and Family Therapy* (1985).

## Drugs and Alcohol

Two recent handbooks addressing drug and alcohol abuse are Blum's *Handbook of Abusable Drugs* (1984), which covers psychotropic drugs and substance abuse, and Hoffmann's *Handbook on Drug and Alcohol Abuse: The Biomedical Aspects* (1983).

## Evaluation Research

Evaluation of social programs and social services is always of interest to social workers and other human services personnel as well as policymakers. Struening and Guttentag's two-volume *Handbook of Evaluation Research* (1975) pulls together a diverse array of theory and research about evaluating social programs, primarily mental health but also public health, preschool education and new careers programs. It covers strategy, design, methodology and data collection in evaluation research in general as well as in specific areas.

## Family and Marital Therapy

Many social workers work with families and are involved in marital counseling. The field is well covered by several handbooks: L'Abate's *Handbook of Family Psychology and Therapy* (1985), which addresses family psychotherapy, as does Gurman's *Handbook of Family Therapy* (1981). Wolman's *Handbook of Family and Marital Therapy* (1983) treats both family psychotherapy and marital psychotherapy. Liberman's *Handbook of Marital Therapy: A Positive Approach to Helping Troubled Relationships* (1980) covers both marriage and family therapy. Sholevar's *Handbook of Marriage and Marital Therapy* (1981) focuses on marriage counseling and family psychotherapy.

## Psychiatry

The field of psychiatry is covered in the previously mentioned encyclopedia *American Handbook of Psychiatry* (1975), edited by Arieti. This six-volume work covers what is known in psychiatry and related fields. The six volumes are (V1) *Foundations of Psychiatry*, (V2) *Child and Adolescent Psychiatry*, (V3) *Sociocultural and Community Psychiatry*, (V4) *Adult Clinical Psychiatry*, (V5) *Organic Disorders and Psychosomatic Medicine and Treatment*, and (V6) *New Psychiatric Frontiers*.

Focusing on narrower aspects of psychiatry are Bernstein's *Handbook of Drug Therapy in Psychiatry* (1983), Hall's *Handbook of Psychiatric Diagnostic Procedures* (1984), and Slaby's *Handbook of Psychiatric Emergencies* (1986).

## Psychology

There are numerous handbooks in the field of psychology. Eysenck's *Handbook of Abnormal Psychology* (1973) covers the broad range of abnormal behaviors. Affective disorders are treated in Paykel's *Handbook of Affective Disorders* (1982). Walker's *Handbook of Clinical Psychology: Theory, Research, and Practice* (1983) focuses on clinical psychology and psychotherapy. Brown covers counseling and applied psychology in his *Handbook of Counseling Psychology* (1984). Barlow's *Clinical Handbook of Psychological Disorders: A Step by Step Treatment Manual* (1985) presents treatment programs for specific psychological disorders. Each chapter is written by an expert in the field.

Working with minorities is covered in Pedersen's *Handbook of Cross-Cultural Counseling and Therapy* (1985) and the six-volume *Handbook of Cross-Cultural Psychology* (1980), edited by Triandis.

Stress, anxiety and depression are the subjects of Kutash's *Handbook on Stress and Anxiety* (1980), Goldberger's *Handbook of Stress: Theoretical and Clinical Aspects* (1982), Beckham's *Handbook of Depression: Treatment, Assessment, and Research* (1985), and Sethi's *Handbook of Organizational Stress Coping Strategies* (1984).

## Psychotherapy

There are several recent handbooks devoted to individual and group psychotherapy. Anchin's *Handbook of Interpersonal Psychotherapy* (1982) focuses on the individual, as do Corsini's *Handbook of Innovative Psychotherapies* (1981) and Garfield's *Handbook of Psychotherapy and Behavior Change: An Empirical Analysis* (1978). Group therapy is treated in Grotjahn's *Handbook of Group Therapy* (1983) and Rosenbaum's *Handbook of Short-Term Therapy Groups* (1983).

Specific types of therapies are the subjects of Ellis' *Handbook of Rational-Emotive Therapy* (1977), Garner's *Handbook of Psychotherapy for Anorexia Nervosa and Bulimia* (1985), Rosewater's *Handbook of Feminist Therapy: Women's Issues in Psychotherapy* (1985), and Wolberg's *Handbook of Short-Term Psychotherapy* (1980).

## Social Services

Demone's *Handbook of Human Service Organizations* (1974) focuses on social services and social work administration, as does Gilbert's *Handbook of the Social Services* (1981). Mental health services and administration are treated in Austin's *Handbook on Mental Health Administration* (1982). Katz addresses services for the handicapped in *Handbook of Services for the Handicapped* (1982). Finally, Rosenblatt covers the field of clinical social work in the *Handbook of Clinical Social Work* (1983), a broad and comprehensive guide presenting major theoretical perspectives, new assessment techniques and intervention strategies, critiques of techniques, current research findings, and overviews of policy issues.

## BIOGRAPHICAL SOURCES

The history of social welfare is filled with many individuals who helped shape American social welfare and social work. An understanding of their lives and the historical forces that shaped modern social work should help contemporary social workers gain a fuller understanding of their own roles.

Social work is often closely allied with other helping professions such as psychology and psychiatry. In addition to the biographical sources on social workers described below, there are several other more general sources for locating biographical information on psychologists, psychiatrists, social scientists and other prominent individuals.

There are basically two different types of biographical sources. Biographical dictionaries are collections of articles on selected individuals and closely approximate encyclopedias by presenting lengthy, scholarly articles that summarize knowledge about the individuals. Biographical directories are compilations of brief information on individuals or institutions. Both types are described below as well as indexes to locating biographical sources.

Trattner's *Biographical Dictionary of Social Welfare* (1986) should probably have been called a biographical encyclopedia. It includes lengthy articles on approximately 300 people who have been important in American social welfare. Its coverage ranges from colonial to fairly recent times. Excluded are living people, persons who were known for their work as elected public officials, all philanthropists, "all those who were primarily abolitionists, feminists, labor union leaders and intellectuals (theorists, writers, educators), as opposed to activists with the exception of some who were exceedingly important in the history of social work education." The editor states that the emphasis is on "doers." The contributors come from a variety of scholarly fields, primarily history and social work. The length and quality of the articles were determined not only by the importance of the individuals but also by the amount of information available. Sources and references are listed at the end of each article.

Another source that contains biographical sketches of important contributors to social welfare and social work is the *Encyclopedia of Social Work*. The new 18th edition contains 99 biographical sketches of persons who made "outstanding contributions" to social welfare and social work.

There are several other general sources of biographical information. *American Men and Women of Science* (1978) is a multivolume reference work providing basic biographical information on American scientists including, in the 13th edition, social and behavioral scientists. The American Psychiatric Association and the American Psychological Association both publish a *Biographical Directory* including such data as training, experience, and specialties.

There are numerous who's whos that list basic biographical data for notable persons. Some that are relevant for social work are *Who's Who in Science* (1968), *World Who's Who of Women* (1987), *Who's Who among Black Americans* (1976 to present), *Who's Who in European Institutions and Organizations* (1983), *Who's Who in Health Care* (1982), *Who's Who of American Women, Who's Who* (1849 to present) and *Who Was Who in America* (1969).

Works for locating biographies include the *Biography Index: A Cumulative Index to Biographical Material and Books and Magazines* (Annual), which serves as an index for locating biographies contained within other works. The *Chicorel Index to Biographies* (1974) lists more than 21,000 entries and provides bibliographic data on book-length biographies. The *Biographical Dictionaries—Master Index* (1976) lists more than 725,000 persons appearing in over 50 who's whos and other collective biographies. The *New York Times Obituaries Index* (v1 1858–1968, v2 1969–1978) serves as a guide to locating obituaries in the *New York Times*.

## DIRECTORIES*

Directories are lists of persons or organizations systematically arranged, usually in alphabetical or classed orders, giving addresses, affiliations, etc., for individuals, and addresses, officers, functions, and similar information for organizations.

Social workers generally perform their work within a formal organization such as a social service agency or mental health clinic. Due to this organizational base social workers often need to consult with persons at another agency or refer clients from one clinic to another. Directories serve the purpose of locating persons or agencies.

Following is a selection of mostly national directories of several types and for various groups. Some may seem dated but they are the most recent editions and should serve at least as starting points for locating persons and services. Regional and local directories are too numerous and diverse to include here. They can be located either through your local library or by consulting the *Directory of Directories* described below. The directories are organized by the group or organization they are intended to serve.

### Aging

The aging population is well served by several directories. The federal government publishes the *Chartbook of Federal Programs on Aging* (1982), which covers such things as social security and housing programs and health services. *Self-Care and Self-Help Groups for the Elderly: A Directory* (1984) provides information about numerous national organizations that are concerned with the elderly or that have programs relevant to older people, their families and health professionals who work with them. Adult day-care centers are listed in the *Directory of Adult Day Care Centers* (1980). The *Directory of Services for the Widowed in the United States and Canada* (Biennial) lists associations, clubs, and agencies which offer counseling and other forms of assistance to widows and widowers. *Administering Aging Programs* (1983) lists municipal and state offices concerned with aging and the aged. The *American Association of Homes for the Aging: Directory of Members*, the *Directory of Nursing Homes in the U.S. and Canada* (Annual) and the *Directory of Nursing Homes* (3rd edition to be published in 1988) thoroughly cover nursing homes and other long-term care facilities.

A publication not restricted to the aged is *Death and Dying: A to Z* (1986). This annual publication covers suicide prevention centers, religious organizations and family counseling services specializing in preparation for and coping with death.

### Associations

Professional social welfare organizations and associations publish numerous directories useful for social workers. For example, the Child Welfare League of America publishes the *CWLA Directory of Member and Associate Agencies* (1985), which includes U.S. and Canadian listings. The Family Service Association of America publishes the *Directory of Member Agencies* (1984), which includes U.S. and Canadian agencies. The National Association of Social Workers publishes the *NASW Register of Clinical Social Workers* (1985), which provides listings of qualified clinical social workers.

Membership directories or rosters are published by other helping professions and organizations, including the American Group Psychotherapy Association (Annual), American Academy of Child Psychiatry (1986), American Academy of Psychoanalysis

---

*This section was originally published in *Encyclopedia of Social Work*, 18th edition, volume 2, pp. 971–977 and is reprinted with the permission of the National Association of Social Workers, Inc., copyright © 1987.

(Biennial), American Association for Marriage and Family Therapy (1987), American Association of Children's Residential Centers (Annual), American Psychiatric Association (1983), American Psychological Association (1985), American Psychoanalytic Association (Biennial), American Society for Adolescent Psychiatry (Biennial), and the Association for the Advancement of Behavior Therapy (Annual). Such rosters and directories are useful for referral purposes. Complete bibliographic details are listed in the bibliographies at the ends of the articles.

## Canada

Many of the directories described above contain sections on Canadian social welfare agencies. Two solely Canadian publications which might prove useful for U.S. social workers are the *Directory of Canadian Human Services* (1983) and *Justice: Directory of Services* (1983).

## Children and Youth Services

Part 1 of the *National Directory of Children and Youth Services* (1984) lists children and youth services alphabetically by state. Part 2, "Who's Who in Federal Children and Youth Services," includes the executive branch and Senate and House committees. Also included are sections on runaway youth centers, resource centers and clearinghouses, national organizations serving children and youth, national city-county guide, and international organizations serving children and youth.

## Criminal Justice

Many social workers work with or in criminal justice organizations. Several directories may be useful. The *Probation and Parole Directory: Adults and Juvenile Probation and Parole Services, United States and Canada* (1981) provides coverage of state agencies, the U.S. Parole Commission and the federal probation system. It is published by the American Correctional Association, which also publishes the *Directory: Juvenile and Adult Correctional Departments, Institutions, Agencies and Paroling Authorities: United States and Canada* (1979) and the *National Jail and Adult Detention Directory* (1983).

## Crisis Intervention

The *National Directory of Hotlines and Crisis Intervention Centers* (1983) lists 889 programs throughout the United States, providing data on program names, addresses, phone numbers, services provided, geographic areas served and target populations.

## Drug Abuse

The National Institute on Drug Abuse publishes the *National Directory of Drug Abuse and Alcoholism Treatment and Prevention Programs* (1983), which lists over 7,500 federal, state, local and privately funded agencies administering or providing drug abuse and alcoholism treatment and prevention services. There is also the *Alcoholism and Drug Abuse Treatment Centers Directory: A Guide to over 9,000 Federal, State, Local and Privately Funded Agencies* (1981), a nonfederal publication.

## Federal and State

A useful federal government publication is the annual *United States Government Manual.* It is the official handbook of the federal government and provides comprehensive information on all branches of government, including quasi-official agencies and international organizations in which the U.S. participates. Entries provide organizational charts, summary statements of each agency's purpose and role, its legislative or executive authority and descriptions of its programs and activities. Complementing the *Manual* is *Government Agencies: The Greenwood Encyclopedia of American Institutions* (1983). Over 100 articles provide overviews of governmental agencies, "their problems, tasks, successes and failures and how they relate to the individual."

State agencies and elected officials are covered in two publications. The *National Directory of State Agencies* (1984) provides easy access by listing state agencies alphabetically by agency functions and by state and includes an appendix listing associations of state government officials. Another state directory is *State Elective Officials and the Legislatures* (1984).

## General

Two general sources should be valuable to persons seeking information about associations and their publications. The *Encyclopedia of Associations* (1985) lists over 18,000 active organizations, including social welfare, legal, public administration, health and medical organizations. It also notes the publications of the listed organizations. A useful source for identifying additional directories is the *Directory of Directories: An Annotated Guide to Business and Industrial Directories, Professional and Scientific Rosters, Directory Databases and Other Lists and Guides of All Kinds* (1985). It lists over 7,800 publications, providing data on frequency of publication, price, editors and addresses. It includes many regional, state and local directories, such as the *Directory of Social and Health Agencies of New York City* (1983), which have not been mentioned in this section.

## International Organizations

To find out about international organizations one may consult the *Yearbook of International Organizations* (1985), which provides information on a wide variety of international organizations and associations. There is also a biennial directory published by the International Association of Schools of Social Work entitled *Directory of Member Schools and Associations.* It includes data on and descriptions of about 500 social work education schools worldwide.

## Mental Health

*The Mental Health Directory* (1985) provides a central source of information on mental health organizations throughout the United States. It includes outpatient mental health clinics, psychiatric hospitals (public and private), and residential treatment centers for emotionally disturbed children. Entries are arranged alphabetically by state and city. The facility type is noted, e.g., psychiatric hospital, outpatient clinic, etc., and the name, address and phone number are provided. Puerto Rico and the Virgin Islands are included. Also included is a listing of state mental health agencies with the names of directors or administrators.

The federal government has also published the *Directory: Federally Funded Community Mental Health Centers* (1981), which lists almost 800 such centers.

## Minority Services

Information useful for aiding minority groups may be found in three directories. *Federal Programs for Minorities, Women and the Handicapped* (1980) is excerpted from the *Catalog of Federal Domestic Assistance* (1980). The *Directory of Financial Aids for Minorities* (1982) lists financial aid programs and awards such as scholarships, fellowships, loans, and grants available to members of minority groups. The *Directory of Special Programs for Minority Group Members: Career Information Services, Employment Skill Banks, Financial Aid Sources* (1986) covers private and governmental agencies offering financial aid, employment assistance and career guidance programs for minorities.

## Public and Private Agencies

Two important and useful directories that are national in scope are the *Public Welfare Directory* (1986) and the *National Directory of Private Social Agencies* (1964). The *Public Welfare Directory* is a useful source of information on public human service programs in the United States and Canada. It is published annually by the American Public Welfare Association and is organized for practical use. It offers information on agencies and key staff and describes public human services offered by federal, state, territorial, county and major municipal agencies. The section on federal agencies describes agencies that have contact with state and local welfare agencies. It also lists personnel, organizational structure, names, addresses and direct-dial phone numbers for key personnel. The section on state agencies describes the administration of public welfare and explains agency jurisdictions. For each state agency it notes "where to write—to whom—and how many copies"—for client inquiries, assistance and services. Organizational structures are also included. There are also sections on Canadian agencies and international social services. Several useful appendices describe in detail national social service programs and offer advice concerning correspondence with state agencies.

Complementing the *Public Welfare Directory* is the *National Directory of Private Social Agencies*. Listing approximately 15,000 agencies, homes and organizations, it includes agencies which provide direct help or make referrals. It lists agencies by services offered as well as alphabetically by state, describing which services are offered and providing names and addresses. Unlike the *Public Welfare Directory* it does not list contact people, organizational structures or any other information. However, it is kept current through monthly supplements, while the *Public Welfare Directory* is published once a year.

Another comprehensive social welfare directory is *Social Service Organizations and Agencies Directory* (1982). It bills itself as "A Reference Guide to National and Regional Social Service Organizations, including Advocacy Groups, Voluntary Associations, Professional Societies, Federal and State Agencies, Clearinghouses and Information Centers." There are 6,700 entries arranged in 47 chapters. All kinds of social service organizations are included, covering services relating to the family, community, substance abuse, law enforcement, the aged, children, youth, women, minorities, etc.

The above-mentioned directories are fairly comprehensive, up-to-date sources of information on organizations and agencies but provide little or no historical information. One source that does is Romanofsky's *Social Service Organizations* (1978). This encyclopedia lists 293 social service organizations that have had a major impact on the social services. Most are national organizations, but prominent local agencies are also included. Most organizations are treated historically.

## Rape Prevention and Treatment

*The National Directory: Rape Prevention and Treatment Resources* (1981) provides access to a diverse array of agencies, organizations and individuals. Entries range from rape crisis centers and community mental health centers to police departments, district attorney offices and individuals who have "expertise in the problems resulting from sexual assault." In addition to United States listings there are entries for Canadian services. Basic data are provided as well as program descriptions.

There are two more directories oriented to helping women. *Surviving Sexual Assault* (1983) is a national directory of rape crisis centers, hotlines and victim assistance programs. It provides text on preventing rape, medical procedures, legal issues, compensation and the psychological consequences of assault. *The Battered Women's Directory* (1985) lists shelters, hotlines, YWCA's, hospitals, etc. which offer services to abused women in the U.S. and abroad.

## Social Services

The *Annual Directory of Management Resources for Community Based Organizations* (1986) lists almost 400 institutions, agencies and firms which will provide some type of management assistance to community-based organizations. The *Directory of Information and Referral Services in the United States and Canada* (1984) lists social service information and referral agencies with one or more staff members who have the exclusive or primary assignment to provide information. *Adoption Agencies, Orphanages and Maternity Homes: An Historical Directory* (1981) covers over 9,200 agencies, both active and closed. The *Directory of Family Planning Grantees, Delegates, and Clinics* (1979) covers over 4,000 family planning clinics and recipients of grants funded by Title X of the Public Health Services Act.

## Suicide

The *Directory of Suicide Prevention/Crisis Intervention Agencies in the United States* (1983) covers approximately 500 suicide prevention and crisis intervention centers. This is a publication of the American Association of Suicidology, which also publishes an annual *Membership Roster* listing professionals involved in suicide prevention.

## Voluntary Organizations

Volunteers and voluntary organizations play an important role in welfare services and social work. Volunteer organizations are covered in the *Community Resources Directory: A Guide to U.S. Volunteer Organizations and Other Resource Groups, Services, Training Events and Courses and Local Program Models* (1984). It purports to be a comprehensive source of information on "*who* is doing *what* for *whom, where*, across the country." It serves as a guide for finding out about volunteer involvement in specific areas of human services. Section 1 lists organizations providing volunteer services and publications devoted to volunteer services. Section 2 covers organizations ranging from colleges and universities to federal and state offices and agencies that provide training programs. Section 3 provides program profiles of organizations providing volunteer services. In addition to covering volunteer organizations, this publication also lists organizations willing to assist volunteer groups for free or for a nominal fee.

There are two more directories of voluntary organizations. One is the *Directory of Agencies: U.S. Voluntary, International Voluntary Intergovernmental* (1975). It provides data on the membership, purposes and programs of more than 300 national and international and intergovernmental agencies in social work and other closely related fields. The second directory is the *Directory of Volunteer Bureaus and Voluntary Action Centers* (1986). The latter title includes name of bureau or center, address, name of executive director, population of community served, organization, structure, and affiliations for 375 member bureaus and centers. It is arranged geographically.

## SOURCES DISCUSSED

### General Sources

Ryder, Dorothy E. *Canadian Reference Sources: A Selective Guide.* 2nd edition. Ottawa: Canadian Library Association, 1981.
Sheehy, Eugene P. *Guide to Reference Books.* 10th edition. Chicago: American Library Association, 1986.
Walford, Albert J. *Walford's Guide to Reference Material.* 4th edition. London: Library Association, 1980.
Webb, William H. *Sources of Information in the Social Sciences: A Guide to the Literature.* 3rd edition. Chicago: American Library Association, 1986.

### Bibliographies

Besterman, Theodore. *A World Bibliography of Bibliographies and Bibliographical Catalogues, Calendars, Abstracts, Digests, Indexes, and the Like.* 4th revised edition. Lausanne: Societas Bibliographica, 1965–66.
*Bibliographic Index: A Cumulative Bibliography of Bibliographies.* New York: H. W. Wilson, 1938 to present.
*Books in Print.* New York: R. R. Bowker. Annual.
Conrad, James H. *Reference Sources in Social Work: An Annotated Bibliography.* Metuchen, New Jersey: Scarecrow, 1982.
*Standard Periodical Directory.* New York: Oxbridge Communications. Annual.
*Ulrich's International Periodical Directory.* New York: R. R. Bowker. Annual with supplements.

### Dictionaries

American Psychiatric Association. *A Psychiatric Glossary: The Meanings of Terms Frequently Used in Psychiatry.* 5th edition. Waltham, Massachusetts: Little, Brown, 1981.
Barker, Robert L. *The Social Work Dictionary.* Silver Spring, Maryland: National Association of Social Workers, 1987.
Clegg, Joan. *Dictionary of Social Services, Policy and Practice.* 3rd edition. London: Bedford and the National Council of Social Service, 1980.
Fisher, Richard B. *The Dictionary of Mental Health.* New York: Granada, 1980.
Mitchell, G. Duncan. *A New Dictionary of Sociology.* London: Routledge and Kegan Paul, 1979.
Timms, Noel and Rita Timms. *Dictionary of Social Welfare.* Boston: Routledge and Kegan Paul, 1982.

### Encyclopedias

Arieti, Silvano, editor. *American Handbook of Psychiatry.* 2nd edition. 6 volumes. New York: Basic Books, 1975.
Corsini, Raymond J., editor. *Encyclopedia of Psychology.* 4 volumes. New York: Wiley, 1984.
Eidelberg, Ludwig, editor-in-chief. *Encyclopedia of Psychoanalysis.* New York: Free, 1968.

Hegel, Carl, editor-in-chief. *Encyclopedia of Management.* 3rd edition. New York: Van Nostrand Reinhold, 1982.

Kadish, Sanford H., editor-in-chief. *Encyclopedia of Crime and Justice.* 4 volumes. New York: Free, 1983.

Kruskal, William H. and Judith M. Tanur, editors. *International Encyclopedia of Statistics.* 2 volumes. New York: Free, 1978.

Kuper, Adam and Jessica Kuper, editors. *The Social Science Encyclopedia.* Boston: Routledge and Kegan Paul, 1985.

National Association of Social Workers. *Encyclopedia of Social Work.* 18th edition. 3 volumes. Silver Spring, Maryland: National Association of Social Workers, 1986.

Romanofsky, Peter, editor. *Social Service Organizations.* 2 volumes. Westport, Connecticut: Greenwood, 1978.

Sills, David L., editor. *International Encyclopedia of the Social Sciences.* 17 volumes. New York: Macmillan, 1968.

Wolman, Benjamin B., editor. *International Encyclopedia of Psychiatry, Psychology, Psychoanalysis, and Neurology.* 12 volumes. New York: Van Nostrand Reinhold, 1977.

Woody, Robert H., editor. *Encyclopedia of Clinical Assessment.* 2 volumes. San Diego, California: Jossey-Bass, 1981.

## Handbooks

### Aging

Binstock, Robert H. and Ethel Shanas, editors. *Handbook of Aging and the Social Sciences.* 2nd edition. New York: Van Nostrand Reinhold, 1985.

Birren, James E. and R. Bruce Sloane, editors. *Handbook of Mental Health and Aging.* Englewood Cliffs, New Jersey: Prentice-Hall, 1980.

Birren, James E. and K. Warner Schaie, editors. *Handbook of the Psychology of Aging.* 2nd edition. New York: Van Nostrand Reinhold, 1985.

Busse, Ewald W. and Dan G. Blazer. *Handbook of Geriatric Psychiatry.* New York: Van Nostrand Reinhold, 1980.

Cohen, Lilly, editor. *Funding in Aging: Public, Private and Voluntary.* 2nd edition. Garden City, New York: Adelphi University Press, 1979.

Finch, Caleb L. and Leonard Hayflick, editors. *Handbook of the Biology of Aging.* New York: Van Nostrand Reinhold, 1977.

Holmes, Monica B. *Handbook of Human Services for Older Persons.* New York: Human Sciences, 1979.

Monk, Abraham, editor. *Handbook of Gerontological Services.* New York: Van Nostrand Reinhold, 1985.

Norback, Craig and Peter Norback. *The Older Americans Handbook.* New York: Van Nostrand Reinhold, 1979.

Palmore, Erdman B., editor. *Handbook on the Aged in the United States.* Westport, Connecticut: Greenwood, 1984.

Schick, Frank L., editor. *Statistical Handbook on Aging Americans.* Phoenix, Arizona: Oryx Press, 1986.

*Sourcebook on Aging.* 2nd edition. Chicago: Marquis Academic Media, Marquis Who's Who, 1979.

### Assessment

American Psychiatric Association. Task Force on Nomenclature and Statistics. *Diagnostic and Statistical Manual of Mental Disorders.* 3rd edition. Washington, DC: American Psychiatric Association, 1980.

Ciminero, Anthony R., Karen S. Calhoun, and Henry E. Adams, editors. *Handbook of Behavioral Assessment.* 2nd edition. New York: Wiley, 1986.

Goldstein, Gerald and Michel Husen, editors. *Handbook of Psychological Assessment.* New York: Pergamon, 1984.
Groth-Marnet, Gary. *Handbook of Psychological Assessment.* New York: Van Nostrand Reinhold, 1984.
Kellerman, Henry and Anthony Burry. *Handbook of Psychodiagnostic Testing: Personality Analysis and Report Writing.* New York: Grune and Stratton, 1981.
Webb, Linda J. et al., editors. *DSM III Training Guide for Use with the American Psychiatric Association's Diagnostic and Statistical Manual of Mental Disorders.* 3rd edition. New York: Brunner/Mazel, 1981.

## Behavior Therapy and Behavior Modification

Fisher, Joel and Harvey L. Gochros, editors. *Handbook of Behavior Therapy with Sexual Problems.* New York: Pergamon, 1977.
Goldstein, Alan and Edna B. Foa, editors. *Handbook of Behavioral Interventions: A Clinical Guide.* New York: Wiley, 1980.
Herson, Michael and Alan S. Bellack, editors. *Handbook of Clinical Behavior Therapy with Adults.* New York: Plenum, 1985.
Leitenberg, Harold, editor. *Handbook of Behavior Modification and Behavior Therapy.* Englewood Cliffs, New Jersey: Prentice-Hall, 1976.
Matson, Johnny L. and John R. McCartney. *Handbook of Behavior Modification with the Mentally Retarded.* New York: Plenum, 1981.
Turner, Samuel M. et al., editors. *Handbook of Clinical Behavior Therapy.* New York: Wiley, 1981.

## Childhood and Adolescence

Adelson, Joseph, editor. *Handbook of Adolescent Psychology.* New York: Wiley-Interscience, 1980.
Bernstein, Norman R. and James Sussex, editors. *Handbook of Psychiatric Consultation with Children and Youth.* New York: SP Medical and Scientific Books, 1984.
Malmquist, Carl P. *Handbook of Adolescence: Psychopathology, Antisocial Development, Psychotherapy.* New York: J. Aronson, 1978.
Mussen, Paul, editor. *Handbook of Child Psychology.* 4th edition. New York: Wiley, 1983.
Ollendick, Thomas H. and Michel Hersen, editors. *Handbook of Child Psychopathology.* New York: Plenum, 1983.
Osofsky, Joy D., editor. *Handbook of Infant Development.* New York: Wiley-Interscience, 1979.
Pravder, Marsha et al., editors. *Handbook of Adolescents and Family Therapy.* New York: Gardner, 1985.
Sgroi, Suzanne M., editor. *Handbook of Clinical Intervention in Child Sexual Abuse.* Lexington, Massachusetts: Lexington Books, 1981.
Walker, C. Eugene and Michael C. Roberts, editors. *Handbook of Clinical Child Psychology.* New York: Wiley, 1983.

## Drugs and Alcohol

Blum, Kenneth. *Handbook of Abusable Drugs.* New York: Gardner, 1984.
Hoffmann, Frederick G. *Handbook on Drug and Alcohol Abuse: The Biomedical Aspects.* 2nd edition. New York: Oxford University Press, 1983.

## Evaluation Research

Struening, E.L. and M. Guttentag, editors. *Handbook of Evaluation Research.* Beverly Hills, California: Sage, 1975.

## Family and Marital Therapy

Gurman, Alan S. and David P. Kniskern, editors. *Handbook of Family Therapy.* New York: Brunner/Mazel, 1981.

L'Abate, Lucianio, editor. *Handbook of Family Psychology and Therapy.* Homewood, Illinois: Dorsey, 1985.

Liberman, Robert P. *Handbook of Marital Therapy: A Positive Approach to Helping Troubled Relationships.* New York: Plenum, 1980.

Sholevar, G. Pirooz, editor. *The Handbook of Marriage and Marital Therapy.* Jamaica, New York: Spectrum Publications, 1981.

Wolman, Benjamin B. and George Stricker, editors. *Handbook of Family and Marital Therapy.* New York: Plenum, 1983.

## Psychiatry

Arieti, Silvano, editor. *American Handbook of Psychiatry.* 2nd edition. 6 volumes. New York: Basic Books, 1975.

Bernstein, Jerrold G. *Handbook of Drug Therapy in Psychiatry.* Boston: J. Wright, 1983.

Hall, Richard C. W. and Thomas P. Beresford, editors. *Handbook of Psychiatric Diagnostic Procedures.* New York: SP Medical and Scientific Books, 1984.

Slaby, Andrew Edmund. *Handbook of Psychiatric Emergencies.* 3rd edition. New Hyde Park, New York: Medical Examination Publishing, 1986.

## Psychology

Barlow, David A., editor. *Clinical Handbook of Psychological Disorders: A Step by Step Treatment Manual.* New York: Guilford, 1985.

Beckham, Ernest E. and William R. Leber, editors. *Handbook of Depression: Treatment, Assessment, and Research.* Homewood, Illinois: Dorsey, 1985.

Brown, Steven D. and Robert W. Lent, editors. *Handbook of Counseling Psychology.* New York: Wiley, 1984.

Eysenck, Hans Jurgen, editor. *Handbook of Abnormal Psychology.* 2nd edition. San Diego, California: R. R. Knapp, 1973.

Goldberger, Leo and Shelomo Breznitz, editors. *Handbook of Stress: Theoretical and Clinical Aspects.* New York: Free, 1982.

Kutash, Irwin L. and Louis B. Schlesinger, editors. *Handbook on Stress and Anxiety.* San Francisco: Jossey-Bass, 1980.

Paykel, E. S., editor. *Handbook of Affective Disorders.* Edinburgh, New York: Churchill Livingstone, 1982.

Pedersen, Paul, editor. *Handbook of Cross-Cultural Counseling and Therapy.* Westport, Connecticut: Greenwood, 1985.

Sethi, Amarjit Singh and Randell S. Schuler, editors. *Handbook of Organizational Stress Coping Strategies.* Cambridge, Massachusetts: Ballinger, 1984.

Triandis, Harry C. et al., editors. *Handbook of Cross-Cultural Psychology.* Boston: Allyn and Bacon, 1980.

Walker, C. Eugene, editor. *Handbook of Clinical Psychology: Theory, Research and Practice.* Homewood, Illinois: Dow Jones-Irwin, 1983.

## Psychotherapy

Anchin, Jack C. and Donald J. Kiesler, editors. *Handbook of Interpersonal Psychotherapy.* New York: Pergamon, 1982.

Corsini, Raymond J., editor. *Handbook of Innovative Psychotherapies.* New York: Wiley, 1981.

Ellis, Albert and Russell Grieger. *Handbook of Rational-Emotive Therapy.* New York: Springer Publishing, 1977.

Garfield, Sol L. and Allen E. Bergin, editors. *Handbook of Psychotherapy and Behavior Change: An Empirical Analysis.* 2nd edition. New York: Wiley, 1978.
Garner, David M. and Paul E. Garfinkel, editors. *Handbook of Psychotherapy for Anorexia Nervosa and Bulimia.* New York: Guilford, 1985.
Grotjahn, Martin. *Handbook of Group Therapy.* New York: Van Nostrand Reinhold, 1983.
Rosenbaum, Max, editor. *Handbook of Short-Term Therapy Groups.* New York: McGraw-Hill, 1983.
Rosewater, Lynne B. and Lenore E. A. Walker, editors. *Handbook of Feminist Therapy: Women's Issues on Psychotherapy.* New York: Springer Publishing, 1985.
Wolberg, Lewis R. *Handbook of Short-Term Psychotherapy.* New York: Thieme-Stratton, 1980.

## Social Services

Austin, Michael J. and William E. Hershey, editors. *Handbook on Mental Health Administration.* San Francisco, CA: Jossey-Bass, 1982.
Demone, Harold W. *Handbook of Human Service Organizations.* New York: Human Sciences, 1974.
Gilbert, Neil and Harry Specht, editors. *Handbook of the Social Services.* Englewood Cliffs, New Jersey: Prentice-Hall, 1981.
Katz, Alfred H. *Handbook of Services for the Handicapped.* Westport, Connecticut: Greenwood, 1982.
Rosenblatt, Aaron and Diana Waldfogel, editors. *Handbook of Clinical Social Work.* San Francisco, CA: Jossey-Bass, 1983.

## Biographical Sources

*American Men and Women of Science.* 13th edition. Lancaster, Pennsylvania: Science, 1978.
American Psychiatric Association. *Biographical Directory of Fellows and Members.* New York: R. R. Bowker, 1941 to present.
American Psychological Association. *Biographical Directory.* Washington, DC: American Psychological Association, 1916 to present.
*Biographical Dictionaries-Master Index.* 3 volumes. Detroit, Michigan: Gale Research, 1975–1976.
*Biography Index.* New York: H. W. Wilson, 1946 to present.
Chicorel, Marietta. *Chicorel Index to Biographies.* 2 volumes. New York: Chicorel Library Publishing, 1974.
Kay, Ernest, editor. *World Who's Who of Women.* Cambridge: Melrose, 1973 to present.
Matney, William C. *Who's Who among Black Americans.* Lake Forest, Illinois: Who's Who among Black Americans, 1976 to present.
*New York Times Obituaries Index.* 2 volumes. New York: Time. V1, 1858–1968, V2, 1969–1978.
Trattner, William I., editor. *Biographical Dictionary of Social Welfare in America.* Westport, Connecticut: Greenwood, 1986.
*Who Was Who in America, 1607–1968.* 4 volumes. Chicago: Marquis Who's Who, 1969.
*Who's Who.* Boston: St. Martin's Press, 1849 to present.
*Who's Who in European Institutions and Organizations.* Chicago: Marquis Who's Who, 1983.
*Who's Who in Health Care.* 2nd edition. Rockville, Maryland: Aspen Systems, 1982.
*Who's Who in Science.* Chicago: Marquis Who's Who, 1968.
*Who's Who of American Women.* Chicago: Marquis Who's Who, 1987.
*World Who's Who of Women.* Chicago: Marquis Who's Who, 1987.

## Directories

### *Aging*

American Association of Homes for the Aging. *Directory of Members.* Washington, DC: American Association of Homes for the Aging. Annual.

American Association of Retired Persons. *Directory of Services for the Widowed in the United States and Canada.* Washington, DC: American Association of Retired Persons. Biennial.

Bleckman, Isaac, editor. *Death and Dying: A to Z.* New York: Croner Publications, 1986.

McKnight Medical Communications. *Directory of Nursing Homes in the United States and Canada.* Northfield, Illinois: McKnight Medical Communications. Annual.

Mongeau, Sam, editor. *Directory of Nursing Homes.* 3d ed. Phoenix, Arizona: Oryx Press, 1988.

Schechter, Irma, editor. *Chartbook of Federal Programs on Aging.* Bethesda, Maryland: Care Reports, 1982.

United States Conference of Mayors. *Administering Aging Programs.* Washington, DC: United States Conference of Mayors, 1983.

U.S. Department of Health and Human Services. Health Care Financing Administration. *Directory of Adult Day Care Centers.* Washington, DC: GPO, 1980.

U.S. Department of Health and Human Services. National Institute on Aging. *Self-Care and Self-Help Groups for the Elderly: A Directory.* Washington, DC: GPO, 1984.

### *Associations*

American Academy of Child Psychiatry. *Membership Directory.* Washington, DC: American Academy of Child Psychiatry, 1986.

American Academy of Psychoanalysis. *Membership Roster.* New York: American Academy of Psychoanalysis. Biennial.

American Association for Marriage and Family Therapy. *Membership Directory.* Washington, DC: American Association for Marriage and Family Therapy, 1987.

American Association of Children's Residential Centers. *Directory of Organizational Members.* Washington, DC: American Association of Children's Residential Centers. Annual.

American Group Psychotherapy Association. *Membership Directory.* New York: American Group Psychotherapy Association. Annual.

American Psychiatric Association. *Biographical Directory.* Washington, DC: American Psychiatric Association, 1983.

American Psychoanalytic Association. *Roster.* New York: American Psychoanalytic Association. Biennial.

American Psychological Association. *Biographical Directory.* Washington, DC: American Psychological Association, 1985.

American Society for Adolescent Psychiatry. *Membership Directory.* Wallingford, Pennsylvania: American Society for Adolescent Psychiatry. Biennial.

Association for the Advancement of Behavior Therapy. *Membership Directory.* New York: Association for the Advancement of Behavior Therapy. Annual.

Child Welfare League of America. *CWLA Directory of Member and Associate Agencies.* New York: Child Welfare League of America, 1985.

Fenton, Joan, compiler. *Directory of Member Agencies.* New York: Family Service Association of America, 1984.

National Association of Social Workers. *NASW Register of Clinical Social Workers.* 4th edition. Silver Spring, Maryland: National Association of Social Workers, 1985.

### *Canada*

Canadian Association for the Prevention of Crime. *Justice: Directory of Services.* Ottawa: Canadian Association for the Prevention of Crime, 1983.

Canadian Council on Social Development. *Directory of Canadian Human Services.* Ottawa: Canadian Council on Social Development, 1983.

## Children and Youth Services

Child Protection Report. *National Directory of Children and Youth Services.* Washington, DC: CPR Directory Services, 1984.

## Criminal Justice

American Correctional Association. *Directory: Juvenile and Adult Correctional Departments, Institutions, Agencies and Paroling Authorities: United States and Canada.* College Park, Maryland: American Correctional Association, 1979.

American Correctional Association. *National Jail and Adult Detention Directory.* College Park, Maryland: American Correctional Association, 1983.

American Correctional Association. *Probation and Parole Directory: Adult and Juvenile Probation and Parole Services: United States and Canada.* College Park, Maryland: American Correctional Association, 1981.

## Crisis Intervention

Myers, John P., editor. *National Directory of Hotlines and Crisis Intervention Centers.* Mullica Hill, New Jersey: Evaluation Research Associates, 1983.

## Drug Abuse

*Alcoholism and Drug Abuse Treatment Centers Directory.* Santa Monica, California: Ready Reference, 1981.

U.S. Department of Health and Human Services. National Institute on Drug Abuse. *National Directory of Drug Abuse and Alcoholism Treatment and Prevention Programs.* Washington, DC: GPO, 1983.

## Federal and State

Council of State Governments. *State Elective Officials and the Legislatures.* Lexington, Kentucky: Council of State Governments, 1984.

Office of the Federal Register. National Archives and Records Administration. *United States Governmental Manual.* Washington, DC: GPO, 1985.

Whitnah, Donald R., editor. *Government Agencies: The Greenwood Encyclopedia of American Institutions.* Westport, Connecticut: Greenwood, 1983.

Wright, Nancy D. and Gene P. Allen, compilers. *The National Directory of State Agencies.* Arlington, Virginia: Information Resources, 1984.

## General

Community Council of Greater New York. *Directory of Social and Health Agencies of New York City.* New York: Columbia University Press, 1983.

Ethridge, James M., editor. *Directory of Directories.* 3rd edition. Detroit, Michigan: Gale Research, 1985.

Gruber, Katherine, editor. *Encyclopedia of Associations.* Detroit, Michigan: Gale Research, 1987.

## International Organizations

International Association of Schools of Social Work. *Directory of Member Schools and Associations.* Vienna, Austria: International Association of Schools of Social Work, 1985.

Union International Associations. *Yearbook of International Associations.* New York: K. G. Saur, 1985.

## Mental Health

U.S. Department of Health and Human Services. National Institute of Mental Health. *Directory: Federally Funded Community Mental Health Centers.* Rockville, Maryland: GPO, 1981.

U.S. Department of Health and Human Services. National Institute of Mental Health. Compiled by Warsade, M. R. et al. *Mental Health Directory.* Washington, DC: GPO, 1985.

## Minority Services

ABC-Clio Information Services. *Directory of Financial Aids for Minorities.* Santa Barbara, California: ABC-Clio Information Services, 1982.

Johnson, Willis L., editor. *Directory of Special Programs for Minority Group Members.* 4th edition. Garrett Park, Maryland: Garrett Park Press, 1986.

U.S. Department of Health and Human Services. National Institutes of Health. *Catalog of Federal Domestic Assistance.* Washington, DC: GPO, 1980.

U.S. Department of Health and Human Services. National Institutes of Health. *Federal Programs for Minorities, Women and the Handicapped.* Washington, DC: GPO, 1980.

## Public and Private Agencies

Croner, Helga B., compiler. *National Directory of Private Social Agencies.* Queens Village, New York: Croner Publications, 1964.

Kruzas, Anthony T., editor. *Social Service Organizations and Agencies Directory.* Detroit, Michigan: Gale Research, 1982.

Romanofsky, Peter, editor. *Social Service Organizations.* Westport, Connecticut: Greenwood, 1978.

Weinstein, Amy, editor. *Public Welfare Directory.* Washington, DC: Public Welfare Association, 1986.

## Rape Prevention and Treatment

Grossman, Rachael. *Surviving Sexual Assault.* New York: Congdon and Weed, 1983.

U.S. Department of Health and Human Services. National Center for the Prevention and Control of Rape. *National Directory: Rape Prevention and Treatment Resources.* Washington, DC: GPO, 1981.

Warrior, Betsy. *Battered Women's Directory.* 9th edition. Cambridge, Massachusetts: Betsy Warrior, 1985.

## Social Services

Alliance of Information and Referral Systems. *Directory of Information and Referral Services in the United States and Canada.* Indianapolis, Indiana: Alliance of Information and Referral Systems, 1984.

Niles, Reg. *Adoption Agencies, Orphanages and Maternity Homes: An Historical Directory.* Garden City, New York: Phileas Deigh, 1981.

Peebles, Marvin L., editor. *Annual Directory of Management Resources for Community Based Organizations.* Philadelphia, Pennsylvania: MLP Enterprises, 1986.

U.S. Department of Health and Human Services. National Clearinghouse for Family Planning Information. *Directory of Family Planning Grantees, Delegates, and Clinics.* Rockville, Maryland: GPO, 1979.

## Suicide

American Association of Suicidology. *Directory of Suicide Prevention/Crisis Intervention Agencies in the United States.* Denver, Colorado: American Association of Suicidology, 1983.

American Association of Suicidology. *Membership Roster.* Denver, Colorado: American Association of Suicidology, 1987 (annual).

## Voluntary Organizations

Association of Volunteer Bureaus. *Directory of Volunteer Bureaus and Voluntary Action Centers.* Green Valley, Arizona: Association of Volunteer Bureaus, 1986.

Kipps, H. C., editor. *Community Resources Directory.* 2nd edition. Detroit, Michigan: Gale Research, 1984.

National Association of Social Workers. *Directory of Agencies: U.S. Voluntary, International Voluntary, Intergovernmental.* Silver Spring, Maryland: National Association of Social Workers, 1975.

# CHAPTER 3
# Journal and Newspaper Articles

This chapter explains how to expeditiously find articles contained within journals. The role of indexes and abstracts as finding tools is the primary focus. Newspaper indexes are also included. Some characteristics of the journal literature are examined. Chapter 4, "Social Work and Related Journals," provides additional detail on the characteristics of the journal literature.

There are at least three dozen scholarly journals specifically devoted to some aspect of social work. In addition to the social work journals there are hundreds more in psychology, sociology, economics, public affairs, political science and other social and behavioral sciences that contain information relevant for social work. Scholarly journals in social work and related fields contain the most current information on many topics. They are more current than books because journal articles generally do not take as long to write and to be published as do books. However, keep in mind that once an article is submitted to a journal it may take three months or longer to be reviewed and at least as long to be published.

Another determining factor in the usefulness of the journal literature is the fact that before an article is published in a scholarly journal, it is usually read by two or more reviewers (members of the editorial board or persons chosen by the editor) who are experts in the area covered in the paper being reviewed. They determine whether or not the article is worthy of publication, that is, whether it is original, makes a contribution to the discipline, and meets commonly agreed upon standards of scholarship. Thus, much of the journal literature has been screened to some extent prior to publication.

## THE OVERABUNDANCE OF JOURNALS

Because there are so many journals, with more coming into existence each year, it is often a difficult task to locate pertinent articles needed for literature reviews or to learn more about a particular subject in order to write a report, term paper, book, etc.

Many persons will begin looking for articles by going to the shelves in the library where journals are kept and starting to browse through a journal that looks like it might have the right kind of articles. While there is nothing wrong with scanning journals, it is a very slow and time-consuming way to find articles on a specific subject. Many scholarly journals are published only four times a year and contain anywhere from four or five to a dozen articles on a variety of topics that fall within the primary focus of a particular journal. It might be necessary to look through many years of a journal to locate what you want.

## INDEXES

Fortunately, it is not necessary to use the browsing method for locating journal articles. Most scholarly (and popular) journals are routinely indexed in indexing services. An index is a systematically arranged list giving enough information about each item to enable it to be identified and traced. Indexes are specialized bibliographic tools that help collect or organize many subjects and academic disciplines to enable the relatively quick retrieval of information. They are another form of reference book. Some indexes are published by professional organizations while others are commercial ventures. Indexes provide the basic bibliographic information necessary to locate an article. Bibliographic information for journal articles includes author(s), title of article, name of journal, volume, issue, pages, and year. An example might look like this:

> Randall, Jack; Gates, Roberta; Schaeffer, Tom. "The Importance of the Psychiatric Team." *Journal of Social Science Literature* 12 (2): 18–25, 1987.

## ABSTRACTS

Some indexing services go one step further and provide summaries (abstracts) of the indexed articles. Some abstracts describe what is in the article while others analyze and indicate the usefulness of the article. In any case, an abstracting service is generally more useful than a simple index. An index without abstracts provides little more than the title of the article to tell you what it is about, and titles in social science journals do not always accurately indicate what the articles cover. Reading an abstract first will often save you from looking up articles that, from the index titles, seem pertinent but under closer scrutiny are not.

A bibliographic citation with an abstract looks like this:

> Randall, Jack; Gates, Roberta; Schaeffer, Tom. "The Importance of the Psychiatric Team." *Journal of Social Science Literature* 12 (2): 18–25, 1987.
>
> Mental Health Division, Willowlawn Hospital, Willowlawn, Arizona.
>
> The importance of teamwork to the functioning and success rate of the psychiatric team is discussed. Patients with a variety of problems proved to benefit from input from a variety of psychiatric professionals. In addition, the professionals themselves benefited from receiving feedback from their colleagues.

There are different kinds of indexing and abstracting services. The most common contain subject and author indexes. An alphabetized subject arrangement is used to bring together many different articles from numerous journals. Thus, you do not have to look through countless journals to find a few articles on a topic. Instead, you merely look in the appropriate index. And if abstracts are included so much the better. Most subject indexes and abstracts include alphabetized author indexes. Some indexes and abstracts also include geographical indexes, while others are arranged by key word in title, in which the initial word of a heading or subheading is indexed.

Publication schedules for indexes and abstracts vary. Most are published quarterly, but some are published biweekly, monthly, semiannually or annually. Even for those indexes published biweekly or monthly there will obviously be a lag between the publication of an article and its citation in an index or abstract.

## PRINT VERSUS ONLINE

With computer databases proliferating and computer searches an everyday occurrence, you may wonder why you would need to use a printed index or abstract. Many of the databases described in Chapter 5 are similar to the indexes and abstracts described in this chapter. However, some indexes and abstracts are not available in electronic form. It is also somewhat expensive to pay for computer searches. Many times you will have to wait for an appointment for a computer search, and then you will be dependent on the skills of the searcher to retrieve what you need.

Using an index or abstract yourself allows for more independent judgement and generally shows you how the literature of a particular discipline is organized. Using a print source can be almost as quick as a computer search if you need only a few recent articles. And when you are browsing through an index you may locate other interesting articles for future reading. But perhaps the best reason, especially for students, is to see how the literature of various disciplines is organized and accessed. Knowing how to do it yourself is usually better than having it done for you.

## WHICH INDEX TO USE

Guides to the literature such as those mentioned in Chapter 1 are often useful for locating the correct index or abstract. But guides are often dated and will not include new publications, nor are they always comprehensive. While there is often more than one indexing or abstracting service for any discipline, indexes for the same subjects are usually grouped together in a library's reference area.

It is advisable to familiarize yourself with the indexes and abstracts pertinent to your area of study or research. Read the preface or introduction to find out its scope and the way it should be used. Most publish a list of journals that they index, and it is useful to compare the lists. Some indexes cover only selected journals for one academic discipline while others are comprehensive in their coverage. Another way to determine which source to use is to ask a reference librarian for advice. You may save yourself a lot of time.

## CUMULATIVE EDITIONS

Also keep in mind that most indexes and abstracts that are published more than once a year have either cumulative volumes or cumulative indexes at the end of the last issue for a year. Such a cumulative index covers a whole year, so you will not have to look through the indexes of individual issues.

## SOURCES REVIEWED

There are numerous indexing and abstracting services in the social and behavioral sciences. The following is a selection of such services that contain information relevant for social work. Keep in mind that there are many indexes and abstracts for subjects not covered here.

### Aging

*Current Literature on Aging,* published quarterly by the National Council on Aging, indexes and annotates selected journal articles and books dealing with aging and such related topics as housing, social welfare and community services, institutional care, health and employment. Each issue contains about 150 entries.

## Business

The monthly *Business Periodicals Index* is a surprisingly useful source for locating materials on the welfare state in scholarly business and economics journals. There are no abstracts.

## Children

*Child Development Abstracts and Bibliography* is published three times a year by the Society for Research in Child Development. It presents approximately 1,200 abstracts each year from almost 190 journals. The focus is on general experimental, social, and clinical psychology; biology; public health; medicine; and education. It includes author and subject indexes.

## Criminal Justice

The *Criminal Justice Periodical Index,* published three times per year, covers journals, digests, and bulletins published in the U.S. that are concerned with various criminal justice and law enforcement topics. There are no abstracts. *Criminal Justice Abstracts* (Quarterly) contains lengthy abstracts of criminal justice articles and reports and is worldwide in scope. *Criminology and Penology Abstracts* (Quarterly) and *Police Science Abstracts* (Quarterly) are also both international in coverage. The latter two are published in The Netherlands and provide good coverage of the European literature.

## Education

A large, comprehensive indexing and abstracting service in education is the Educational Resources Information Center (ERIC) system. ERIC is comprised of several clearinghouses around the U.S. that collect, store and disseminate educational materials. Because its coverage is so broad, there is much material of interest to social workers, especially those involved in school social work. Collected materials are abstracted and the indexes and abstracts are published in two parts: (1) an index to educational journals, *Current Index to Journals in Education* (Monthly) and (2) an index to other types of materials, such as research reports, *Resources in Education* (Monthly). The materials in the latter source are available on microfiche, and many libraries serve as depositories for the microfiche collection. Journal articles are not reproduced on microfiche.

While not as comprehensive as the ERIC system, the *Education Index,* published 10 times per year, provides subject and author coverage of over 300 educational journals. Although there are no abstracts, a handy feature is the index to book reviews found in the back of each issue.

## Family

*Sage Family Studies Abstracts* (Quarterly) provides access to journal articles and books, pamphlets, government publications and legislative research studies concerned with family studies. Broad subject categories cover lifestyles, life cycles, marital and family processes, problems, therapy and counseling, sex roles, social issues, etc. About 250 abstracts are included in each issue.

The *Inventory of Marriage and Family Literature* (Annual) is a comprehensive index to all aspects of marriage and family studies. It utilizes a key-word index. Its former title was *International Bibliography of Research in Marriage and the Family.*

## Multidisciplinary

The *Social Sciences Index* (Quarterly) is a multidisciplinary index, without abstracts, covering major journals from most social and behavioral sciences. Its social welfare coverage is good, and because it is multidisciplinary it provides a variety of perspectives. There is also an index to reviews of social science books.

Another multidisciplinary index is the *Social Sciences Citation Index,* published three times a year by the Institute for Scientific Information (ISI). This is an international multidisciplinary index covering what ISI considers to be the core journal literature in each social and behavioral science discipline, including social work. It is divided into three parts: (1) *Permuterm Subject Index,* (2) *Source Index,* and (3) *Citation Index.* When looking for articles on a social work topic, start with the *Permuterm Subject Index.* Look under the appropriate topic and you will find listed names of persons who have published on that topic during the year the index covers. Next look up the name in the *Source Index* for the same year. The *Source Index* will contain the bibliographic information needed to locate the document. Although there are no abstracts, the *Source Index* includes, in addition to the bibliographic citation, the bibliography or references the author used to write the article. This is an easy way to obtain a bibliography. It also allows the researcher to identify key names in a given subject by showing whose work the author built upon. In a sense it takes you back in time.

The *Citation Index* takes you forward in time. To find out who may have read a particular article and cited it in his or her bibliography, look up the name of the author in the *Citation Index* for the following years. It will show you who cited the article and in which journal, providing an easy way to discover who has cited whom and built upon the works of others. Remember it takes a year or two for new articles to be cited by other scholars. An article that has been frequently cited indicates that it had an impact in its area. *SSCI* also indexes book reviews.

## Newspapers

Most major newspapers are indexed. The *New York Times Index* provides detailed subject indexing of one of the country's leading newspapers. It is published semimonthly, with an annual cumulation. The *Wall Street Journal Index* is published monthly, with an annual cumulation. The *London Times* is covered in the *Official Index,* a bimonthly with semiannual cumulations. The MicroPhoto Division of Bell and Howell has published indexes to such newspapers as the *Christian Science Monitor, Los Angeles Times, Chicago Tribune* and the *Washington Post.*

There are also two computerized databases for newspapers. The National Newspaper Index, available through Dialog, indexes the *New York Times, Wall Street Journal, Washington Post, Christian Science Monitor* and the *Los Angeles Times.* With the exception of the *New York Times Index,* none of the above has abstracts.

A computerized database that provides the full text of newspaper articles is VuText. It was developed by the *Philadelphia Enquirer.* It includes the text of articles from newspapers around the country.

## Psychology

One of the most important sources of information for social workers is *Psychological Abstracts,* published monthly by the American Psychological Association. It covers the world's literature in psychology and related disciplines, including social work, and is close to being comprehensive. Each issue is organized into major classification categories. One section of particular interest to social workers is "Treatment and Prevention." Monthly issues are cumulated twice a year (January–June and July–December). The brief subject and author indexes that appear in each monthly issue are also cumulated twice a year.

When you look up a subject in the brief subject index in the back of each monthly issue you will find an abstract entry number to look up in the main part of the text. The abstracts are numbered sequentially, and when you look up the abstract entry number, you will find the bibliographic citation and abstract.

The semiannual cumulations are easier to use than each monthly issue. When you look up a subject in the semiannual indexes you will find, in addition to the abstract entry number, the major five or six concepts that describe each indexed article. They are like an abstract of the abstract, allowing you to scan many different studies before having to look them up in the text volumes.

A compilation of the indexing vocabulary in *Psychological Abstracts* is published in the *Thesaurus of Psychological Index Terms,* presently in its fourth edition. The *Thesaurus* serves as a guide for determining which terms to look up in *Psychological Abstracts.*

## Public Affairs

Social workers are often involved in the public policymaking process, and social research is frequently utilized for policymaking. The public policy and affairs literature can aid social workers in participating in the political arena and in formulating policy. The public policy and affairs literature will also contain policy evaluation research or program evaluation research. Evaluation research assesses, in a deliberate and structured manner, the impact of a program of social intervention to determine if the consequences do indeed fulfill the expectations of the policy makers.

An excellent index to the public affairs and policy literature is the *Public Affairs Information Service Bulletin (PAIS)*. *PAIS* is published semimonthly, which makes it an excellent current awareness source. It is selective in what it indexes (there are no abstracts) and attempts to select the most authoritative journal articles, books, pamphlets, government documents and reports of public and private agencies that relate to economic and social conditions, public administration and international relations.

*Human Resources Abstracts* covers the literature in human and social problems and solutions. This quarterly covers topics which include the labor force, employment and unemployment, work life, income distribution and maintenance, industrial and labor relations, career development, slum rehabilitation, minority group problems and rural poverty. It is published by Sage Publications.

Sage also publishes *Sage Urban Studies Abstracts* which covers a broad range of topics on urban affairs, such as urban planning and land use, transportation and communication, housing and social services, and social, economic, and political conditions. A complementary index is *Urban Affairs Abstracts,* published weekly by the National League of Cities. It attempts to be an up-to-date guide to the most relevant urban literature on a host of topics. Like the Sage publications it has subject and author indexes. Unlike the others, it contains a geographic index.

A good political science index is the annual *United States Political Science Documents (USPSD)*. *USPSD* indexes and abstracts articles from core political science journals. The abstracts are lengthy. *Sage Public Administration Abstracts: An International Information Service* is a quarterly publication that indexes articles, books, pamphlets and government publications on public administration.

## Social Work

There are three major indexing and abstracting services that cover the social work and social welfare literature. The primary source is *Social Work Research and Abstracts* (*SWRA*), published quarterly by the National Association of Social Workers. Prior to its inception there was no single source of indexing and abstracting devoted to social work. The inauguration of *Abstracts for Social Workers* (the original title) in 1965 was a significant development in social work, for it began the integration of a previously disparate and fragmented profession by starting a trend toward a common knowledge base for all social work practice. The *Abstracts* pulled together social work knowledge. This source provided a single medium in which practitioners and educators were able to follow new developments in the diagnosis and treatment of social problems. The original editors also believed that "the formulation of a classification scheme should help break the barrier, hitherto insurmountable, of codifying social work literature."

In the late 1970s a decision was made to change the editorial focus of the *Abstracts*. The summer 1977 edition appeared with a new title (*Social Work Research and Abstracts*) and a new emphasis on publishing original research articles as well as abstracts of previously published articles. According to its editors, manuscripts to be published would be concerned with "social work technology, research strategies and methods of research as applied to problems faced by social workers, theoretical articles that have relevance to social work research activities, and analytical reviews of the research." NASW's new emphasis on lengthy and technical reports of research has filled a gap often found in other social work journals.

*SWRA* has maintained this editorial focus to the present day. Each issue contains from two to half a dozen articles devoted to research on a topic of reasonably broad concern to social workers and has review articles. Following the articles are two short sections, "Research Briefs" and "Research Notes." "Research Briefs" describes studies currently in progress. Its intention is to allow readers to keep abreast of research developments as they are occurring. "Research Notes" presents short reports of research findings and ideas that would not normally be publishable as full-length articles.

Following the research section are the abstracts. Approximately 200 journals are reviewed each year and the articles abstracted. In addition to journals devoted to social work, journals from allied fields, such as psychology, psychiatry, counseling and community mental health are covered. The abstracts are divided into sections, with "Fields of Service" being the major one. About 400 abstracts are included in each issue. The winter issue, which is the final issue of the year, includes annual subject and author indexes. It also has an index to the research articles published in *SWRA*.

In addition to *SWRA* there are two, more narrowly focused, indexes. One is the *Journal of Human Services Abstracts,* published quarterly by Project Share. It provides abstracts of articles and documents concerned with the management of human services. Project Share is operated for the Office of the Assistant Secretary for Planning and Evaluation, Department of Health and Human Services, by Aspen Systems. Project Share defines itself as a clearinghouse for improving the management of human services. Its purpose is to "acquire, evaluate, store and make available a broad range of documentation on subjects of concern, interest, and importance to those responsible for the planning, management and delivery of human services." Emphasis is given to collecting and disseminating information concerned with the integration of services at the delivery level.

Project Share documents are drawn from a variety of sources, including state publications and technical reports prepared by the federal government, research institutes and private companies. The following information is provided for each document: author, title, date, pagination, availability, document order number, price and format. The preface describes how to order a document. Author, title and subject indexes provide access. Cumulative indexes appear in the final issue of the year. This service is a particularly good source for locating hard-to-find information about the management and delivery of human services.

*Social Welfare, Social Planning/Policy and Social Development: An International Database* is published by Sociological Abstracts. It is issued in tripartite form, with each section focusing on one segment of the title: Section 1, "Social Welfare"; Section 2, "Social Planning/Policy"; and Section 3, "Social Development." This abstracting service presents broad coverage of the applied social sciences including policy studies, welfare administration, evaluation research, social work, health administration, and community organization. Each issue includes a table of contents and author, subject and source indexes. It is not cumulated annually.

## Sociology

*Sociological Abstracts (SA)* is a large and comprehensive abstracting service published five times a year by Sociological Abstracts. *SA* is a collection of nonevaluative abstracts of the world's sociological literature. It covers most substantive areas in sociology and related disciplines and includes abstracts of papers delivered at conferences. Each issue contains subject, author and source indexes. The final issue, appearing in December, includes cumulative annual indexes. As previously noted, Sociological Abstracts also publishes *Social Welfare, Social Planning/Policy and Social Development.* The overlap in journal coverage between the two indexes is minimal.

## Women's Studies

One abstracting source that focuses on women is *Women Studies Abstracts,* a quarterly publication. It was founded in order to aid the research into and understanding of women's contributions to society. It is a guide to the literature concerned with women and covers such topics as education and socialization, sex roles and characteristics, family, employment, mental and physical health, pregnancy, childbirth, family planning, and abortion. Not all of the indexed materials (journal articles, books, reports, etc.) are abstracted, but many are. There are annual indexes.

## CONCLUSION

There are many other indexes and abstracts. Some are discussed in other parts of this book. Many others are not mentioned because they are too far removed from social work and social welfare. If you do need to research fields such as anthropology or economics or medicine, consult one of the guides to the literature mentioned in the chapter on reference books or consult with a reference librarian who can help you choose an appropriate source.

## SOURCES DISCUSSED

### Aging

National Council on Aging. *Current Literature on Aging,* 1957 to present. Washington, DC: National Council on Aging. Quarterly. Online equivalent: None.

## Business

Business Periodicals Index. New York: H. W. Wilson, 1958 to present. Monthly with frequent cumulations. Online equivalent: None.

## Children

Society for Research in Child Development. *Child Development Abstracts and Bibliography.* Chicago: Society for Research in Child Development, 1927 to present. Triannually. Online equivalent: None.

## Criminal Justice

*Criminal Justice Abstracts,* 1968 to present. Monsey, New York: Willow Tree. Quarterly. Online equivalent: None.

*Criminal Justice Periodical Index,* 1975 to present. Ann Arbor, Michigan: University Microfilms International. Triannually. Online equivalent: Criminal Justice Periodical Index, available through Dialog.

Kugler for Criminologica Foundation. *Criminology and Penology Abstracts,* 1961 to present. Deventer, The Netherlands: Kugler for Criminologica Foundation. Bimonthly. Online equivalent: None.

Kugler for Criminologica Foundation. *Kugler for Criminologica Foundation. Police Science Abstracts,* 1973 to present. Deventer, The Netherlands: Kugler for Criminologica Foundation. Bimonthly. Online equivalent: None.

## Education

*Current Index to Journals in Education,* 1969 to present. Phoenix, Arizona: Oryx Press. Monthly with semiannual cumulations. Online equivalent: ERIC, available through BRS, Dialog.

*Education Index,* 1929 to present. New York: H. W. Wilson. Monthly except July and August with annual cumulations. Online equivalent: Education Index, available through Wilsonline.

U.S. Department of Education. National Institute of Education. *Resources in Education,* 1966 to present. Washington, DC: GPO. Monthly with semiannual cumulations. Online equivalent: ERIC, available through Dialog, BRS.

## Family

Aldrus, Joan and Nancy Dahl, editors. *International Bibliography of Research in Marriage and Family,* 1900–1972. Minneapolis, Minnesota: University of Minnesota Press in association with the Institute of Life Insurance. Online equivalent: None.

Olsen, David and Nancy Dahl, editors. *Inventory of Marriage and Family Literature, 1973 to present.* St. Paul, Minnesota: University of Minnesota Press. Annual. Online equivalent: None.

*Sage Family Studies Abstracts,* 1979 to present. Beverly Hills, California: Sage. Quarterly. Online equivalent: None.

## Multidisciplinary

Institute for Scientific Information. *Social Sciences Citation Index,* 1969 to present. Philadelphia, Pennsylvania: Institute for Scientific Information. Triannually with annual cumulation. Online equivalent: Social SciSearch, available through Dialog, BRS.

*Social Sciences Index,* 1974 to present. New York: H. W. Wilson. Quarterly. Online equivalent: Social Sciences Index available through Wilsonline.

## Newspapers

*National Newspaper Index,* 1979 to present. Belmont, California: Information Access. Online
  equivalent: National Newspaper Index, available through Dialog (also available on
  microfilm).
*New York Times Index,* 1913 to present. New York: New York Times. Online equivalent:
  National Newspaper Index, available through Dialog (also available on microfilm).
*Times* (London). *Official Index,* 1906 to present. London: The Times. Online equivalent:
  None.
*Wall Street Journal Index,* 1958 to present. New York: Dow Jones. Online equivalent:
  National Newspaper Index, available through Dialog (also available on microfilm).

## Psychology

American Psychological Association. *Psychological Abstracts,* 1927 to present. Washington,
  DC: American Psychological Association. Monthly with semiannual cumulations.
  Online equivalent: PsycInfo, available through Dialog, BRS.
American Psychological Association. *Thesaurus of Psychological Index Terms.* 4th edition.
  Washington, DC: American Psychological Association, 1986.

## Public Affairs

*Human Resources Abstracts: An International Information Service,* 1966 to present. Beverly
  Hills, California: Sage. Quarterly. Online equivalent: None.
National League of Cities/U.S. Conference of Managers. *Urban Affairs Abstracts,* 1971 to
  present. Washington, DC: National League of Cities/U.S. Conference of Mayors. Week-
  ly. Online equivalent: None.
*Public Affairs Information Service Bulletin,* 1915 to present. New York: PAIS. Semimonthly
  with 3 quarterly and one annual cumulations. Online equivalent: PAIS, available
  through Dialog, BRS.
*Sage Public Administration Abstracts: An International Information Service,* 1974 to present.
  Beverly Hills, California: Sage. Quarterly. Online equivalent: None.
*Sage Urban Studies Abstracts,* 1973 to present. Beverly Hills, California: Sage. Quarterly.
  Online equivalent: None.
University of Pittsburgh. University Center for International Studies. *United States Political
  Science Documents,* 1975 to present. Pittsburgh, Pennsylvania: University Center for
  International Studies, University of Pittsburgh. Annual. Online equivalent: USPSD,
  available through Dialog.

## Social Work

National Association of Social Workers. *Social Work Research and Abstracts,* 1965 to
  present. Albany, New York: National Association of Social Workers, Inc. Quarterly.
  Online equivalent: Social Work Abstracts, available through BRS.
Project Share. *Journal of Human Services Abstracts,* 1976 to present. Rockville, Maryland:
  Project Share. Irregular. Online equivalent: None.
Sociological Abstracts. *Social Welfare, Social Planning/Policy and Social Development: An
  International Database,* 1979 to present. San Diego, California: Sociological Abstracts,
  Semiannual, no annual cumulations. Online equivalent: SOPODA, available through
  Dialog, BRS.

## Sociology

Sociological Abstracts. *Sociological Abstracts,* 1952 to present. San Diego, California: Sociological Abstracts. 5 times a year. Online equivalent: Sociological Abstracts, available through BRS, Dialog.

## Women's Studies

Women Studies Abstracts. *Women Studies Abstracts,* 1972 to present. Rush, New York: Women Studies Abstracts. Quarterly. Online equivalent: None.

# CHAPTER 4
# Social Work and Related Journals*

This chapter examines the journal literature of social work and social welfare. An explanation of the importance of the journal literature and its role in scholarly communication is presented. A brief literature review discusses research concerning the content of social work journals. Practice and educational changes affecting the profession of social work and their consequences for its literature are explained. Finally, a selection of relevant journals is presented and discussed. See Chapter 3 for an explanation on how best to access the primary journal literature through the use of secondary sources such as indexing and abstracting sources.

## ROLE OF SCHOLARLY JOURNALS

Journals on social welfare and social work constitute perhaps the most important body of literature for practitioners, educators and students. There are several reasons for this. Journals are the primary vehicles for reporting research and constitute the foundation of knowledge in any scholarly discipline or professional practice based on scholarship. Journals form the core of scholarly and professional communication.

Scholarly journals publish research reports that focus on problems which lend themselves to systematic, detailed observations. Such problems are usually very specific, narrowly defined questions which can be encompassed in a single investigation. The typical research report published as a journal article attempts to answer relevant questions by the examination of pertinent evidence or data which are presented in the article. The articles must follow a generally agreed upon outline for presenting evidence. There should be a brief introductory statement of the current state of knowledge concerning the question under investigation. This introduction may mention what others have said about the problem and point out the gaps or contradictions in the existing knowledge. It should note the question or problem being examined and how it relates to the gaps or contradictions in the literature.

The article should then describe the method of analysis to be used and why the method will yield valid answers. The data and facts generated by the methodology, such as a questionnaire, are then explained in relation to the problem being investigated. Finally, there is a statement of how well the data and analysis have answered the question or solved the problem. Suggestions for further research may be made in the conclusion.

Other types of articles in scholarly journals are either theoretical articles or reviews. In a theoretical article the author attempts to place what is known in a theoretical

*Parts of this chapter were originally published as "Social Work Journals: A Review," *Serials Review* 8(1) (Spring 1982): 9–13, and are reprinted with the permission of Pierian Press.

framework useful for explaining or predicting social (or scientific) phenomena. Review articles also examine what is known, usually by a comprehensive exposition of the literature on the subject. However, review articles do not always use a theoretical framework.

The bulk of scholarly journals are composed of research papers. Scholarly journals are aimed at specialists in a given field and are the primary means of communication among the specialists. Books may also report original research but generally take longer to write and to be published than do journal articles.

## REFEREE SYSTEM

Another feature of journals that contributes to them being the primary means of scholarly communication is the referee system. Editors of journals are not usually full-time journalists but rather distinguished scholars in the discipline or content area to which the journal is devoted. The editors are assisted by an editorial board, also composed of distinguished scholars. The editorial board and other scholars who volunteer their services read papers submitted to the journal to decide whether or not the papers are appropriate for publication. Scholarly papers may or may not be solicited by the journal editor. Most scholarly journals do not solicit articles unless the editors are planning a thematic issue. A few journals do, however, publish only solicited articles.

In any event, papers are screened by reader-specialists selected by the editor. Frequently, the names of the authors are removed from the papers in order to avoid bias in the course of evaluation. The readers comment on the scholarship, writing style and appropriateness of the paper's content for the particular journal to which it was submitted. The paper is then returned to the editor with suggestions to either publish it as is, return it to the author for revisions before it can be published, or reject it. If a paper is rejected by one journal it can be resubmitted to another, and usually is.

This referee system, for better or worse, acts as a screening device and attempts to ensure a journal's quality. The content of books do not always receive this same scrutiny until after they have been published and are then reviewed by specialists. Most scholarly journal articles are written by academics, and this is usually the case in social work. Practitioners do contribute to the literature but to a lesser extent. Academics are under pressure from their employing institutions to publish and contribute to their discipline's literature. This publish or perish syndrome has caused a proliferation of new journals as more and more scholars seek to publish. The proliferation of social work journals has been dramatic in recent years.

## LITERATURE REVIEW

Before examining the structural changes that have affected the journal literature, it is appropriate to find out what has been written about the contents of social work journals.

Weinberger and Tripodi (1969) examined selected social work journals from the years 1956–1965. They found the number and percentage of research articles increasing over time and increasing emphasis on empirical research and less speculation about research. Taber and Shapiro (1965) analyzed the content of selected social work journals through 1963. They looked for evidence of change in the contents of the literature over time and found an increasing emphasis on "empiricality" and reliable or verifiable knowledge. Half of the empirical material dealt with practice experience. The authors noted an increasing emphasis on generalized experience and a decrease in reports of personal experience. They found "references to theories and concepts increased many times over from the 1920's to the 1950's." However, they point out that theory and content were used for exposition with little emphasis on revision of concepts or development of systematic theory. Research reports were scarce and not related to theory. They noted that half the authors were practitioners and a third were social work educators.

Picking up where Taber and Shapiro left off, Howe and Schuerman (1974) examined trends in the social work literature from 1957–1972. They found a general decline in the number of social treatment articles. There was a corresponding increase in policy, administration, service delivery, and client-oriented behavior articles. Increased theoretical diversity was found in the treatment literature.

Jayaratne (1979) analyzed five primary journals for evidence of empiricism and to discern author affiliations. He found that only a few articles were empirical (reported original research) and that the percentage has not changed meaningfully in two decades. He found a fairly even distribution between academic and nonacademic social workers' contributions to the literature, although the distribution was influenced by the type of journal.

Lindsey (1978) examined the operation of professional journals in social work, concentrating on editorial boards, their characteristics and criteria influencing decision making. He compared the editorial boards of social work journals with those of psychology and sociology. One important difference was the much greater emphasis on qualitative research rather than quantitative methods. Social work editorial board members also suffered by comparison with those of sociology and psychology in terms of the excellence and volume of their own published works. Despite the fact that they serve as gatekeepers to the literature, the editorial board members themselves have little personal experience with publishing. Lindsey's strongest criticism of social work journals is his statement that "social work has emerged with editorial boards controlling the major professional journals with a view toward remedial education, entertainment, and reaching the widest circulation."

Kirk and Rosenblatt (1980) examined the contribution of women to social work journals. They examined five major journals from 1934 to 1977: *Smith College Studies in Social Work, Child Welfare, Social Casework, Social Service Review* and *Social Work*. The authors found that although women dominate the social work profession numerically, they are underrepresented as authors of articles. From 1934 through the 1960s, the proportion of women authors in social work journals declined. However, since 1969, the percentage of articles published by women has increased.

## STRUCTURAL CHANGES AFFECTING THE LITERATURE IN SOCIAL WORK

The profession of social work has undergone several changes in professional education and practice in the past two decades that have affected the quantity and scope of the professional literature in the discipline, particularly the journal literature. In order to understand the current thrust of social work literature it is necessary to understand the recent changes in the practice of and education for social work.

Siporin (1978) refers to the traditional model of social work education and practice as the "old paradigm." In the "old paradigm" there were eight basic elements to social work education that were commonly and officially accepted within the profession. They were the "primary helping methods" of casework, group work and community organization; the "supporting methods" of administration and research; and the "supporting knowledge areas" of public welfare, psychiatric information and psychological information.

The traditional organizational scheme of social work began to change as society changed. It goes without saying that the 1960s were a period of social change, and the tumultuous events had their effect on social work education, practice and literature. Social work had to cope with the influx of public monies into the profession from the Great Society social programs and with demands for new services. Civil rights, the Great Society antipoverty and welfare programs, self-help and consciousness-raising groups, new standards and restrictions on institutionalization and the consequent release into the community of previously institutionalized persons, and the antiwar movement all affected the education, practice and literature of social work.

With greater demands being placed on social work by a society seeking solutions to its problems, the profession began to rethink its mission and methods of educating its members, striving for a greater degree of professionalism and becoming more academic and research oriented. Schools of social work moved away from established curricula, placing greater emphasis on administration, planning and research. In addition, there was emphasis on social problems, e.g., mental impairment, gerontology, child abuse, and deinstitutionalization. A host of new treatment methods developed as a response to the wider array of social problems faced by social work than in the past. Curricula still tend, however, to be organized to some extent around the basic areas of social work methods, human behavior and environment, social welfare history and policy, and research and field practice.

Social work educational programs increased in numbers at all levels of higher education. Before 1950 there were only two doctoral programs in social work: at Bryn Mawr and Chicago (*Encyclopedia of Social Work*, pp. 290–300). In 1971 there were 20 doctoral programs, today 37. However, most professional social work education occurs at the master's degree level. The master of social welfare is generally considered the terminal professional degree. According to a publication by the Council on Social Work Education issued in July 1980, there were 46 schools with accredited master's degree programs prior to 1960. As of July 1980, there were 87 accredited master's degree programs.

Another indicator of the growth in the quantity of social workers and the trend toward professionalization is the increase in baccalaureate programs designed to prepare beginning professional practitioners for entry-level positions in social service agencies. Those with postbaccalaureate degrees would be freed from routine work demanding a lower level of skill. The Council on Social Work Education began accrediting baccalaureate programs in 1974. As of July 1980, there were 274 undergraduate programs in social work, including those in preaccreditation status.

Thus, concomitant with a changing society were changes in social work education and practice. Academic social work programs grew in numbers as did the number of social workers teaching in academe. The increased number of social workers and social work teachers seeking to publish caused a need for additional outlets, mechanisms such as professional journals. Social work began to seek an academic knowledge base of its own through the development and publishing of social work journals.

## TRADITIONAL SOCIAL WORK JOURNALS

Social work journals are periodical publications directed primarily toward social work practitioners, educators and scholars. The articles are usually written by social workers or those in closely allied professions. The editorial boards of social work journals are composed primarily of either social work practitioners or educators.

Prior to the 1970s there were relatively few journals exclusively concerned with social work. This may reflect a historical trend in social work as a practice profession with an emphasis on practical rather than academic skills. Social work was conducted in a variety of institutions related to welfare, health, education and justice. For example, there was little emphasis from within the profession on research or theory building; what little empirical research was published was often conducted by a small number of academic social workers rather than by practitioners. Although this appears to still be the norm, the trend in the literature is toward greater emphasis on empirical research and theory building.

Only seven of the major social work journals started before 1950 are in existence today. Of these, five were published by associations while only two were academic in origin. The five association journals are *Social Casework,* begun in 1920 by the Family Service Association of America; *Child Welfare,* founded in 1922 by the Child Welfare League of America; *Journal of Jewish Communal Service,* founded in 1923 by the Conference of Jewish Communal Services; *Public Welfare,* inaugurated in 1943 and published by the American Public Welfare Association; and *Social Worker/ LaTravailleur,* begun in 1932 by the Canadian Association of Social Workers. *Social Service Review* is a University of Chicago Press publication which began in 1927. *Smith College Studies in Social Work* was started in 1930.

## PROLIFERATION OF NEW JOURNALS

Not until the late 1950s did the number of social work journals increase substantially. The National Association of Social Workers founded *Social Work* in 1956. The International Council on Social Welfare founded *International Social Work* in 1958. The *Journal of Education for Social Work* was established by the Council on Social Work Education in 1965. In 1965 the NASW began the first indexing and abstracting service devoted exclusively to social work, *Abstracts for Social Workers.* The Graduate School of Social Work at Boston College started *Urban and Social Change Review* in 1967.

The British Association of Social Workers began *British Journal of Social Work* in 1971. The NASW established *Health and Social Work* in 1976, *Practice Digest* and *Social Work in Education* in 1978. *Administration in Social Work* was begun by Haworth Press in 1977. By the 1970s more social science concepts found their way into social work thinking, and the social problem-oriented research of sociology no doubt was utilized more extensively by social work, resulting in the *Journal of Sociology and Social Welfare* in 1973. The *Journal of Social Welfare* also started in 1973. Another research journal, *Journal of Social Service Research,* began in 1977. *Clinical Social Work Journal* began publication in 1973. Established in 1975, *Social Thought* is published by the National Conference of Catholic Charities. *Social Work with Groups* started in 1978.

The problem-oriented approach in social work is also reflected in the establishment of *Health and Social Work* (1973), *Social Work in Health Care* (1975), *Child and Youth Services* (1977), and *Journal of Gerontological Social Work* (1978).

Several new journals are oriented toward particular groups of practitioners. Examples are *Clinical Gerontologist* (1977), *Clinical Supervisor* (1982), *Hospice Journal* (1985) and *Pediatric Social Work* (1980).

One more event worth mentioning was the change in emphasis in one of NASW's major publications. In 1977, *Abstracts for Social Workers,* recognizing the trend toward research and publication, changed its name to *Social Work Research and Abstracts* and its emphasis to the scientific accumulation of knowledge through studies and reviews of research and scientific strategies and methods pertaining to social work.

No longer merely an abstracting and indexing service, it publishes research articles as well as abstracts.

Scholarly journals vary in the quality and quantity of their articles. It is up to the reader to determine which ones present useful materials.

## JOURNALS REVIEWED

The rest of this chapter is devoted to listing and briefly describing the 100 most pertinent journals either devoted to or related to the study and practice of social work and social welfare. When the journal was begun; the sponsoring organization, if any; the place of publication and publisher; and the International Standard Serial Number, (ISSN) number are also indicated. ISSN is a unique number assigned to every journal for easier identification. It would be useful to include the ISSN number when subscribing to a journal.

A publication that provides additional information on the journals listed below is Mendelsohn's *An Author's Guide to Social Work Journals*, 2nd edition (1987). It provides information needed by authors preparing manuscripts. Included information covers such areas as journal affiliation, publication frequency, editorial focus, subscription rates and addresses, editor's name and address, number of manuscript copies needed for submission, size of pages, margins, length and spacing, style information, length of review process, publication lag times, and acceptance rates.

*Administration and Society.* Beverly Hills, California: Sage Publications, 1969 to present. Quarterly. ISSN 0095-3997.
This journal publishes empirically oriented research reports and theoretically specific articles which synthesize or contribute to the advancement of understanding and explanation in the fields of public and human service organizations, their administrative processes, and their effect on society.

*Administration in Mental Health.* American College of Mental Health Administration. New York: Human Sciences, 1972 to present. Quarterly. ISSN 0090-1180.
Its aim is to advance the practice, study, and process of administration in the mental health setting. A major objective is to make mental health administration visible as a professional career and field of knowledge.

*Administration in Social Work.* New York: Haworth, 1977 to present. Quarterly. ISSN 0364-3107.
Its mission is to publish theory and practice articles concerned with management and administration in social work and related human service fields.

*Administrative Science Quarterly.* Ithaca, New York: Cornell University, 1956 to present. Quarterly. ISSN 0001-8392.
This quarterly is dedicated to advancing the understanding of administration through empirical investigation and theoretical analysis. Articles cover all types of organizations—business, governmental, educational, health care and military—in environmental and cultural contexts.

*American Journal of Drug and Alcohol Abuse.* American Academy of Psychiatrists in Alcoholism and Addictions. New York: Marcel Dekker, 1974 to present. Quarterly. ISSN 0095-2990.
This publication is dedicated to the presentation of essential aspects of drug and alcohol abuse by established workers in their fields. Provides a medically oriented forum for interchange of ideas between preclinical, clinical, and social modalities involved in the study and treatment of drug abuse and alcoholism.

*American Journal of Family Therapy.* New York: Brunner/Mazel, 1973 to present. Quarterly. ISSN 0192-6187.
This journal publishes articles based on research, clinical practice, theory, and literature reviews concerned with some aspect of family therapy.

*American Journal of Orthopsychiatry.* American Orthopsychiatric Association. Albany, New York: AOA Publications, 1930 to present. Quarterly. ISSN 0002-9432.
This journal publishes scholarly work in the area of clinical practice, research conceptualization, and delivery of therapeutic and social services. Its goal is to synthesize and apply the knowledge base of psychiatry, psychology, social work and related disciplines.

*American Journal of Psychotherapy.* Association for the Advancement of Psychotherapy. New York: Association for the Advancement of Psychotherapy, 1946 to present. Quarterly. ISSN 0002-9564.
This journal publishes articles concerned with all types of psychotherapy.

*Behavior Therapy.* Association for the Advancement of Behavior Therapy. New York: Association for the Advancement of Behavior Therapy, 1970 to present. 5 times a year. ISSN 0005-7894.
This is an interdisciplinary journal that publishes research of an experimental and clinical nature that contributes to the theories, practices and evaluation of behavior therapy or behavior modification.

*Behavioral Assessment.* Association for Advancement of Behavior Therapy. Elmsford, New York: Pergamon, 1979 to present. Quarterly. ISSN 0191-5401.
This is an interdisciplinary journal publishing articles in the areas of assessment, design, methodology, statistics, measurement, and program evaluation regardless of population or setting.

*British Journal of Social Work.* British Association of Social Workers. New York: Academic Press, 1971 to present. 6 times a year. ISSN 0045-3102.
Articles are oriented toward practitioners in a variety of settings. It includes selected abstracts from journals in psychology, sociology, psychiatry, community work, and public and social policy.

*Catalyst: A Socialist Journal of the Social Services.* Institute for Social Service Alternatives. New York: Institute for Social Service Alternatives, 1978 to present. Quarterly. ISSN 0191-040X.
Publishes theoretical and practice articles from a progressive political perspective.

*Child Abuse and Neglect: The International Journal.* International Society for the Prevention of Child Abuse and Neglect. Elmsford, New York: Pergamon, 1977 to present. Quarterly. ISSN 0145-2134.
Provides an international, multidisciplinary forum on the prevention and treatment of child abuse and neglect, including sexual abuse. Its scope also extends to all aspects of life which either favor or hinder optimal family bonding.

*Child and Adolescent Social Work Journal.* New York: Human Sciences, 1983 to present. Quarterly. ISSN 0738-0150.
Its focus is on work with children, adolescents and their parents. Articles deal with clinical treatment, social concerns, problems, research and cultural issues.

*Child and Family Behavior Therapy.* New York: Haworth, 1978 to present. Quarterly. ISSN 0731-7107.
Publishes research, reviews, theoretical case studies, case reports, and technique innovations dealing with children, adolescents or families from a behavioral perspective.

*Child and Youth Services.* New York: Haworth, 1977 to present. Quarterly. ISSN 0145-935X.
Each issue is devoted to a special topic. Articles focus on research-based practice in the specific subarea being covered.

*Child Care Quarterly: A Professional Journal of Day and Residential Child Care Practice.* New York: Human Sciences, 1971 to present. Quarterly. ISSN 0045-6632.
Publishes articles based on practice, research, supervision, administration and policy that are concerned with the improvement of child care practice in a variety of day and residential settings.

*Child Psychiatry and Human Development.* American Association for Psychiatric Services for Children. New York: Human Sciences, 1970 to present. Quarterly. ISSN 0009-398X.
This is an interdisciplinary, international journal that publishes articles concerned with the clinical and normative aspects of human development. The specialties of child psychiatry, pediatrics, child psychology, social work and child development are usually represented in articles devoted to basic and experiential knowledge with a clinical application.

*Child Welfare.* Child Welfare League of America. New York: Child Welfare League of America, 1920 to present. Bimonthly. ISSN 0009-4021.

This is a journal of policy, practice, and program devoted to the needs and goals of personnel associated with the field of child welfare. It covers all phases of child welfare that affect the health, education, and psychosocial needs of children. It reports on innovations in practice, agency administration and board functions, staffing designs and staff education, legislation, research, and community development.

*Children and Youth Services Review.* Children and Youth Services Research Foundation. Elmsford, New York: Pergamon, 1979 to present. Quarterly. ISSN 0190-7409.

Publishes research, theoretical articles, evaluation studies and literature reviews concerned with children and youth services.

*Children Today.* U.S. Department of Health and Human Services. Office of Human Development Services. Washington, DC: GPO, 1954 to present. 6 times a year. ISSN 0361-4336.

Reports on successful programs and practices in fields serving children, youth and families: child welfare, health, mental health, education, day care and social services.

*Clinical Gerontologist: The Journal of Aging and Mental Health.* New York: Haworth, 1977 to present. Quarterly. ISSN 0731-7115.

Publishes articles concerned with practical applications to the assessment of or intervention with mental disorders in later life.

*Clinical Social Work Journal.* National Federation of Societies for Clinical Social Work. New York: Human Sciences, 1973 to present. Quarterly. ISSN 0091-1674.

Publishes articles concerned with the clinical applications of existing theories, especially those that include cases illustrating speculation about theory and research papers with clinical applications.

*The Clinical Supervisor.* New York: Haworth, 1982 to present. Quarterly. ISSN 0732-5223.

This journal is designed to facilitate communication of ideas, experiences, skills, techniques, concerns and needs of supervisors in psychology, psychiatry, social work, education and related disciplines.

*Community Mental Health Journal.* National Council of Community Mental Health Centers. New York: Human Sciences, 1965 to present. Quarterly. ISSN 0010-3853.

Devoted to the broad fields of community mental health theory, practice and research.

*Computers in Human Services.* New York: Haworth, 1984 to present. Quarterly. ISSN 0740-445X.

Publishes all types of articles concerned with existing practices and future potentials of computers and information and assistive technologies in human service. Types of articles include software application descriptions, case studies, research reports, review papers, position papers, and software and book reviews.

*Crisis: International Journal of Suicide and Crisis Studies.* International Association for Suicide Prevention. Toronto: C. J. Hogrefe, 1980 to present. Biannual. ISSN 0227-5910.

In addition to being the association newsletter, it publishes research articles.

*Crisis Intervention.* Crisis Intervention Institute. Buffalo, New York: Crisis Intervention Institute, 1969 to present. Quarterly. ISSN 0045-9046.

Contains articles and reviews on the effectiveness of stress modulation, life/crisis interventions, crisis phone services, evaluations of short-term treatment, theoretical papers on the effects of life crises on personal beliefs and values, self perception and health behavior patterns.

*Current Issues in Psychoanalytic Practice.* Society for Psychoanalytic Training and the New York Center for Psychoanalytic Training. New York: Haworth, 1984 to present. Quarterly. ISSN 0737-7851.

Publishes papers that illuminate facets of transference and countertransference resistance, psychosexual development and unconscious process. It is designed to enhance the diagnostic understanding and therapeutic repertoire of the mental health profession.

*Day Care and Early Education.* New York: Human Sciences, 1973 to present. Quarterly. ISSN 0092-4199.

This journal bills itself as a "practical and lively magazine" aimed at early childhood teachers, program administrators, day care workers and other professionals concerned with the education of young children. Practical curricula, staff development and current issues are addressed.

*Emotional First Aid: A Journal of Crisis Intervention.* American Academy of Crisis Interveners. Southwestern Academy of Crisis Interveners. New York: Brunner/Mazel. Quarterly. ISSN 0739-828X.
Articles address practical applications of crisis management skills and principles.

*Family Relations: Journal of Applied Family and Child Studies.* National Council on Family Relations. St. Paul, Minnesota: National Council on Family Relations, 1952 to present. Quarterly. ISSN 0197-6664.
Reports experiences of practitioners serving family fields through education, counseling, and community services. Evaluates innovative work methods and discusses the application of research and theory to practice.

*Family Therapy.* California Graduate School of Marital and Family Therapy. San Diego, California: Libra Publishers, 1972 to present. Triannual. ISSN 0091-6544.
Publishes articles devoted to the broad field of family and marital therapy.

*The Gerontologist.* Gerontological Society of America. Washington, DC: Gerontological Society of America, 1961 to present. 6 times per year. ISSN 0016-9013.
Publishes articles designed to bring the results of research and innovative practice to its readership of practitioners, planners, administrators, educators, applied researchers and students. Its aim is to enhance the understanding of human aging.

*Group.* Eastern Group Psychotherapy Society. New York: Brunner/Mazel, 1977 to present. Quarterly. ISSN 0362-4021.
Articles concerned with group psychotherapy and group processes and clinical, theoretical, or research based.

*Group and Organizational Studies: An International Journal.* Beverly Hills, California: Sage, 1976 to present. Quarterly. ISSN 0364-1082.
Publishes research articles, research review reports, research and evaluation studies, action research reports and critiques of research, all directed to group facilitators, trainers, educators, consultants, or managers in organizations.

*Health and Social Work.* National Association of Social Workers. Silver Spring, Maryland: National Association of Social Workers, 1976 to present. Quarterly. ISSN 0360-7283.
Publishes articles that describe practice, innovations and research in the field of health and social work.

*The Hospice Journal.* New York: Haworth, 1985 to present. Quarterly. ISSN 0742-969X.
Prefers to publish articles which focus on applied research or evaluation studies, reviews of research, theory or clinical methods, or innovative or improved methods of clinical care and case studies.

*Human Services in the Rural Environment.* Cheney, Washington: Inland Empire School of Social Work and Human Services, 1976 to present. Quarterly. ISSN 0193-9009.
Articles are concerned with all types of issues concerning the delivery of human services in rural areas.

*Indian Journal of Social Work.* Tata Institute of Social Services. Bombay, India: Tata Institute of Social Services, 1940 to present. Quarterly. ISSN 0019-5634.
The articles span a variety of subjects related to social work and applied social services. Articles are both research and practice based.

*Information and Referral: The Journal of the Alliance of Information and Referral.* Alliance of Information and Referral. Indianapolis, Indiana: Alliance of Information and Referral, 1979 to present. Biannual. ISSN 0278-2383.
Publishes practical and theoretical articles on issues related to the impact of information and referral systems on the design and delivery of human services.

*International Journal of Aging and Human Development.* Farmingdale, New York: Baywood Publishing, 1973 to present. 8 times a year. ISSN 0091-4150.
Articles emphasize psychological and social studies of aging and the aged.

*International Journal of Group Psychotherapy.* American Group Psychotherapy Association. New York: International Universities Press, 1951 to present. Quarterly. ISSN 0020-7284.
Devoted to publishing articles concerned with the theory, research and practice of group psychotherapy.

*International Journal of Mental Health.* Armonk, New York: M. E. Sharpe, 1972 to present. Quarterly. ISSN 0020-7411.
Publishes articles on social and community psychiatry, adult and child mental health services, neuropsychology, and psychiatric epidemiology.

*International Social Work.* International Council on Social Welfare. International Association of Schools of Social Work. International Federation of Social Workers. Bombay, India: International Council on Social Welfare, 1958 to present. Quarterly. ISSN 0020-8728.
Publishes articles emphasizing social policy, social welfare, programmers and services, social work practice, education, and research.

*Intervention.* The Professional Corporation of Social Workers of Quebec. Montreal: La Corporation Professionnelle des Travailleurs, 1969 to present. Triannual. ISSN 0047-1321.
Publishes articles by corporation members that share the results of their research and professional experience.

*The Journal for Specialists in Group Work.* Association for Specialists in Group Work. Alexandria, Virginia: American Association for Counseling and Development, 1978 to present. Quarterly. ISSN 0193-3922.
Articles address research, innovations and ideas, and working with groups.

*Journal of Abnormal Child Psychiatry.* Arlington, Virginia: American Psychological Association, 1973 to present. Quarterly. ISSN 0091-0627.
Articles are concerned with research and theory in psychopathology in childhood and adolescence. Emphasizes research-based articles.

*Journal of Child Psychology and Psychiatry.* The Association for Child Psychology and Psychiatry. Elmsford, New York: Pergamon, 1960 to present. Bimonthly. ISSN 0164-1735.
Articles are research papers, reviews, case reports, brief research reports, etc. concerned with theory, research, and clinical practice in child and adolescent psychology, psychiatry, and allied disciplines.

*Journal of Community Psychology.* Brandon, Vermont: Clinical Psychology Publishing, 1973 to present. Quarterly. ISSN 0090-4392.
Publishes articles devoted to research, evaluation, assessment, and intervention and reviews that deal with human behavior in community settings.

*Journal of Contemporary Psychotherapy.* Long Island Institute for Mental Health. New York: Human Sciences, 1970 to present. Biannual. ISSN 0022-0116.
Publishes an eclectic range of papers on psychotherapy, both theoretical and practical.

*Journal of Continuing Social Work Education.* Continuing Education Program. School of Social Welfare. Nelson A. Rockefeller College of Public Affairs and Policy. State University of New York at Albany. Albany: Continuing Education Program, 1981 to present. Irregular. ISSN 0276-0878.
Publishes articles concerned with new developments, issues, problems and research in continuing education, staff development and training in social work. The articles include descriptions of innovative programs, research studies, reviews of the literature and evaluation results.

*Journal of Divorce.* New York: Haworth, 1977 to present. Quarterly. ISSN 0147-4022.
Publishes articles concerned with clinical studies and research in family therapy, family mediation, family studies, and family law.

*Journal of Family Issues.* National Council on Family Relations. Beverly Hills, California: Sage, 1980 to present. Quarterly. ISSN 0192-513X.
Carries research, reviews and syntheses of research findings, and theoretical essays concerned with major family issues.

*Journal of Gerontological Social Work.* Hunter College of the City University of New York. New York: Haworth, 1978 to present. Quarterly. ISSN 0163-4372.
Articles cover a wide range of topics pertaining to social work practice in the field of aging.

*Journal of Homosexuality.* Center for Research and Education in Sexuality. San Francisco State University. New York: Haworth, 1974 to present. ISSN 0091-8369.
Publishes interdisciplinary research on homosexuality and related topics.

*Journal of Independent Social Work,* 1985 to present. Quarterly. Washington, DC: Catholic University, 1974 to present. 8 times a year.
Articles are theoretical, practice oriented, philosophical, or concern issues of interest to social workers who are in private clinical practice or in consulting and proprietary activities.

*Journal of Jewish Communal Service.* Conference of Jewish Communal Service. East Orange, New Jersey: Conference of Jewish Communal Service, 1923 to present. Quarterly. ISSN 0022-2089.
Devoted to articles covering issues and themes concerned with Judaism and communal service.

*Journal of Marital and Family Therapy.* American Association for Marriage and Family Therapy. Washington, DC: American Association for Marriage and Family Therapy. ISSN 0194-472X.
Publishes articles on research, theory and clinical practice and training in marital family therapy.

*Journal of Marketing for Mental Health,* 1986 to present. New York: Haworth, 1975 to present. Biannual. ISSN 0883-7589.
Articles focus on emerging marketing applications for the providers of mental health services.

*Journal of Marriage and the Family.* National Council on Family Relations. St. Paul, Minnesota: National Council on Family Relations, 1939 to present. Quarterly. ISSN 0022-2445.
Articles are on research theory on the family.

*Journal of Offender Counseling, Services and Rehabilitation.* New York: Haworth, 1976 to present. Quarterly. ISSN 0195-6116.
Articles are concerned with the counseling, rehabilitation and services to juvenile and adult offenders.

*Journal of Policy Analysis and Management.* Association for Public Policy Analysis and Management. Durham, North Carolina: Institute of Policy Sciences and Public Affairs, 1981 to present. Quarterly. ISSN 0276-8739.
Articles cover substantive fields of public policy or deal with issues of professional practice in policy analysis and public management.

*Journal of Psychopathology and Behavioral Assessment.* New York: Plenum, 1979 to present. Quarterly. ISSN 0882-2689.
Publishes articles on research, theory, and clinical investigations in psychopathology and behavioral assessment.

*Journal of Psychotherapy and the Family.* New York: Haworth, 1985 to present. Quarterly. ISSN 0742-9703.
Publishes articles geared to the needs of psychotherapists involved in the practice of marital and family therapy. Issues are thematic.

*Journal of Social Work and Human Sexuality.* New York: Haworth, 1981 to present. Triannual. ISSN 0276-3850.
Articles are of interest to social workers involved with the broad range of subjects and concerns pertaining to human sexuality and family planning.

*Journal of Social Work Education.* Council on Social Work Education. Washington, DC: Council on Social Work Education, 1965 to present. 3 times a year. ISSN 0022-0612.
Articles address issues relevant to the education and training of social workers and present innovative approaches to social welfare and social work with educational implications.

*Journal of Sociology and Social Welfare.* West Hartford, Connecticut: University of Connecticut, 1973 to present. Quarterly. ISSN 0191-5096.
Articles analyze social welfare institutions, policies, or problems from a sociological perspective.

*Journal of Volunteer Administration.* Association for Volunteer Administration. Boulder, Colorado: Association for Volunteer Administration, 1982 to present. Quarterly. ISSN 0733-6535.
Presents theoretical and research-based papers that have a practical application and relate to volunteers, volunteering or volunteer management.

*Journal of Youth and Adolescence.* New York: Plenum, 1972 to present. Bimonthly. ISSN 0047-2891.
Multidisciplinary in scope, it publishes research reports, theoretical papers, comprehensive reviews and clinical reports that address themselves to the subject of youth and adolescence.

*Omega: Journal of Death and Dying.* Farmingdale, New York: Baywood Publishing, 1970 to present. Quarterly. ISSN 0030-2228.
Emphasis is on research and theoretical articles concerned with terminal care, individual and social attitudes toward death, suicide, grief, bereavement, mortality, and death as a part of politics and society.

*Paedovita: An International Journal Concerned with the Emotional Well Being of Institutionalized Children.* Oak Brook, Illinois: Eterna, 1984 to present. Quarterly. ISSN 0737-5131.
Publishes all types of articles on the emotional well being of institutionalized children.

*Parenting Studies.* International Society for Research in Parenting. Oak Brook, Illinois: Eterna, 1984 to present. Quarterly. ISSN 0737-5123.
Publishes all types of articles concerned with parenting.
*Pediatric Social Work.* Eterna International. Oak Brook, Illinois: Eterna. ISSN 0195-5926.
Publishes all types of articles concerned with pediatric social work.
*Prevention in Human Services.* New York: Haworth, 1980 to present. Quarterly. ISSN 0270-3114.
Each issue is devoted to in-depth coverage of a specific topic in the field of prevention.
*Psychotherapy.* Division of Psychotherapy, American Psychological Association. Phoenix, Arizona: American Psychological Association, 1963 to present. Quarterly. ISSN 0033-3204.
Publishes theoretical articles, research studies, case reports, discussions of practice and papers focusing on training-related issues.
*Psychotherapy in Private Practice.* New York: Haworth, 1983 to present. Quarterly. ISSN 0731-7158.
Articles are concerned with innovations in clinical methods and assessments, consultation, practice management, psychotherapy, and research related to psychotherapy and psychological test evaluation in private practice.
*The Psychotherapy Patient.* New York: Haworth, 1984 to present. Quarterly. ISSN 0738-6176.
Each issue is thematic. Articles are either theoretical or clinical contributions dealing with patient attributes.
*Public Administration Review.* American Society for Public Administration. Washington, DC: American Society for Public Administration, 1963 to present. Bimonthly. ISSN 0033-3344.
Articles cover the broad spectrum of public administration.
*Public Welfare.* American Public Welfare Association. Washington, DC: American Public Welfare Association, 1943 to present. Quarterly. ISSN 0033-3816.
Publishes articles examining welfare, national social policy issues, reports of significant welfare work, social work theory and public welfare legislation.
*Residential Treatment of Children and Youth.* New York: Haworth, 1982 to present. Quarterly. ISSN 0731-7123.
Covers the field of residential treatment of children and youth, including the community counterparts, from psychiatric hospitals to group care and includes the administrative, clinical, educational, and child-care disciplines.
*School Social Work Journal.* Illinois Association of School Social Workers. Glen Ellyn, Illinois: Illinois Association of School Social Workers, 1976 to present. Biannual. ISSN 0161-5653.
Publishes practice articles applying to social work in the schools.
*Small Group Behavior.* Beverly Hills, California: Sage, 1970 to present. Quarterly. ISSN 0090-5526.
An international and interdisciplinary journal which presents research and theory about all types of small groups, including but not limited to therapy and treatment groups.
*Smith College Studies in Social Work.* Smith College School for Social Work. Northhampton, Massachusetts: Smith College School for Social Work, 1930 to present. 3 times a year. ISSN 0037-7317.
Publishes articles that are theoretical or research reports concerned with clinical social work practice and education.
*Social Casework: The Journal of Contemporary Social Work.* Family Service of America. Milwaukee, Wisconsin: Family Service of America, 1920 to present. Monthly except July and August. ISSN 0037-7678.
Directed primarily to social work practitioners and educators. Articles examine social work theory and practice, report experimentation and research, and address professional concerns of social workers.
*Social Policy.* New York: Social Policy Corporation, 1970 to present. Quarterly. ISSN 0037-7783.
All types of articles on social policy.

*Social Service Review.* School of Social Service Administration, University of Chicago. Chicago, Illinois: University of Chicago Press, 1927 to present. Quarterly. ISSN 0037-7961.
Articles emphasize original research and professional issues in social welfare and public policy.

*Social Thought.* Catholic Charities, U.S.A. and the National Catholic School of Social Service, Catholic University of America. Washington, DC: Catholic Charities U.S.A., 1975 to present. Quarterly. ISSN 0099-183X.
This journal examines contemporary social problems, their impact on society, and social policy and programs from a critical perspective.

*Social Work.* National Association of Social Workers. Silver Spring, Maryland: National Association of Social Workers, 1956 to present. 6 times a year. ISSN 0037-8046.
This publication is devoted to the improvement of practice and the extension of knowledge in social welfare. Articles examine established practices, evaluate new techniques, research current social problems, and critically examine the social work profession.

*Social Work in Education.* National Association of Social Workers. Silver Spring, Maryland: National Association of Social Workers, 1978 to present. Quarterly. ISSN 0162-7961.
This journal focuses on practice, theory and research in the field of social work in elementary and secondary education.

*Social Work in Health Care.* New York: Haworth, 1975 to present. Quarterly. ISSN 0098-1389.
Publishes articles directed to social workers in all sectors of health care.

*Social Work Research and Abstracts.* National Association of Social Workers. Silver Spring, Maryland: National Association of Social Workers, 1965 to present. Quarterly. ISSN 0148-0847.
In addition to being an indexing and abstracting service, it publishes articles concerned with social work technology, research strategies, and methods of research as applied to problems faced by social workers.

*Social Work Today.* British Association of Social Workers. Birmingham, England: British Association of Social Workers, 1970 to present. Weekly. ISSN 0037-8070.
This is a news publication aimed at British social workers.

*Social Work with Groups: A Journal of Community and Clinical Practice.* New York: Haworth, 1978 to present. Quarterly. ISSN 0160-9513.
Articles focus on practice, theoretical conceptualizations, and research findings that contribute to social work with groups.

*The Social Worker/LaTravailleur Social.* Canadian Association of Social Workers. Ottawa: Myropen Publications, 1928 to present. Quarterly. ISSN 0037-8089.
This bilingual publication publishes articles on social work practice methods, policy initiatives in social welfare, legislative developments of relevance to social work and social welfare, as well as research findings.

*Suicide and Life Threatening Behavior.* American Association of Suicidology. New York: Guilford Press, 1971 to present. Quarterly. ISSN 0363-0234.
Devoted to emergent approaches in theory and practice related to self-destructive and other-destructive behaviors.

*The Urban and Social Change Review.* Boston College Graduate School of Social Work Alumni Association. Boston: Boston College, 1967 to present. Semiannual. ISSN 0042-0832.
This is an interdisciplinary journal taking an action-oriented approach to the solution of urban and social problems. Articles attempt to integrate scientific developments and social service practice.

*Women and Health.* New York: Haworth, 1978 to present. Quarterly. ISSN 0363-0242.
Publishes research and review articles, including theoretical models that impinge on the multiple disciplines of women's health.

*Women and Therapy.* New York: Haworth, 1982 to present. Quarterly. ISSN 0270-3149.
This journal is devoted to descriptive theoretical, clinical and empirical perspectives on the topic of women and therapy.

*Youth and Society.* Beverly Hills, California: Sage, 1969 to present. Quarterly. ISSN 0044-118X.
This is an interdisciplinary journal directed at the dissemination of theoretical and empirical knowledge. Articles focus on the study of child and youth socialization.

## REFERENCES

Council on Social Work Education. *Colleges and Universities with Accredited Undergraduate Social Work Programs.* New York: Council on Social Work Education, 1980.

Council on Social Work Education. *Schools of Social Work with Accredited Master's Degree Programs.* New York: Council on Social Work Education, 1980.

Howe, Michael W. and John R. Schuerman. "Trends in the Social Work Literature: 1957–72." *Social Service Review* 48 (June 1974): 279–285.

Jayaratne, Srinika. "Analysis of Selected Social Work Journals and Productivity Rankings among Schools of Social Work." *Journal of Education for Social Work* 15 (Fall 1979): 72–80.

Kirk, Stuart A. and Aaron Rosenblatt. "Women's Contributions to Social Work Journals." *Social Work* 25 (3) (1980): 204–209.

Lindsey, Duncan. "The Operation of Professional Journals in Social Work." *Journal of Sociology and Social Welfare* 5 (1978): 273–298.

Lindsey, Duncan. *The Scientific Publication System in Social Science.* San Francisco: Jossey-Bass, 1978.

Mendelsohn, Henry N. *An Author's Guide to Social Work Journals.* 2nd edition. Silver Spring, Maryland: National Association of Social Workers, 1987.

National Association of Social Workers. *Encyclopedia of Social Work.* 17th edition. Washington, DC: National Association of Social Workers, 1977.

Siporin, Max. "Practice Theory and Vested Interests." *Social Service Review* 52 (September 1978): 418–433.

Taber, Merlin and Iris Shapiro. "Social Work and Its Knowledge Base: A Content Analysis of Periodical Literature." *Social Work* 10 (October 1965): 100–106.

Weinberger, Roslyn and Tony Tripodi. "Trends in Types of Research Reported in Selected Social Work Journals, 1956–65." *Social Service Review* 43 (December 1969): 439–447.

# CHAPTER 5
# Computerized Literature Searches and Databases

This chapter presents an overview of computerized literature searching. A brief history of the development of databases is followed by an explanation of online systems and their relevance for social work education and practice. Examples of computerized literature searches are presented. The coverage of social work and social welfare literature in social science databases is examined. Finally, an alphabetical listing with descriptions of pertinent social and behavioral science databases is given.

## THE INFORMATION EXPLOSION

The proliferation of information in recent years has not only caused problems of keeping up with a particular body of literature but has also made it difficult to expeditiously find information when it is needed. It becomes more and more difficult to find a particular article or report as the volume of social science literature increases.

The need to gain control over the proliferation of social science and science information has been recognized for some time. As a result, a great deal of attention has been given to methods of collecting, storing, and retrieving information. Many different groups and organizations contributed to the development of information processing. Government and industry, librarians and publishers, professional organizations and other groups within scientific and social science disciplines all made an effort to develop means to control information.

## ELECTRONIC DATA PROCESSING

Electronic data processing greatly facilitated the process of indexing. Much greater quantities of information could be collected, stored and retrieved far more rapidly electronically than was possible through manual methods. The recent development of electronic storage and retrieval is illustrated by the fact that prior to 1970, electronic systems were, at best, primitive and not readily available for public use. One of the earliest electronic document storage and retrieval systems was developed by Lockheed to control and retrieve technical documents for the National Aeronautics and Space Administration. The system was successful and met such an important need that Lockheed created a separate company, Lockheed Information Systems, to commercially market electronic storage and retrieval of bibliographic information. Precisely locating a single article or document within a vast body of literature in order to retrieve it for use was, and still is, the primary purpose of electronic storage of bibliographic information.

The swift development of computers after 1970 made it economically feasible to store large volumes of bibliographic information in computerized form. Such bibliographic information is, for practical purposes, expressed in natural language.

The term used to refer to such information sources is "database." A database is a collection of related information that is computer readable. It is possible to interpret the information stored electronically by use of a computer.

## ONLINE SYSTEMS

Today's computer systems are referred to as online systems. An online information retrieval system is a set of computer hardware and software for retrieval of information from databases. The hardware is the physical components of the computer system, such as the electronic storage memories of the computer, the terminals or keyboards used to interact with it, and the screens or printers used to view the results. The software is the group of programs and procedures that act as instructions for the computer system.

Lockheed Information Systems uses a software system called Dialog, and its service is known as Dialog Information Retrieval Service. In addition to Dialog there are Bibliographic Retrieval Service (BRS) and Systems Development Corporation (SDC) all of which provide access to hundreds of databases. These three companies are the largest but by no means the only companies in the information trade. It is important to note that the companies that provide access to databases, for the most part, do not create them. Rather, they serve as vendors for the producers of databases.

## DATABASE PRODUCERS

Database producers are organizations that collect information, selecting items such as journal articles, technical reports, patents, books, conference papers, annual reports, newspaper and magazine articles, government publications, theses, dissertations, and bibliographies for inclusion in their databases. The bibliographic details, and in many cases summaries or abstracts of each document, are keyed into a computer in machine readable form. The data are stored on magnetic tapes or disks. The tapes or disks are often used to produce printed versions of the indexes; however, many databases have no print counterpart.

Database producers may be societies and organizations, such as the National Association of Social Workers, the American Psychological Association, or the American Sociological Association. Many databases are developed by private companies, such as the Institute for Scientific Information, Management Contents, or the BioSciences Information Service. Other databases are produced or funded by the federal government, such as the Educational Resources Information Center (ERIC), produced by the National Institute of Education; National Technical Information Service (NTIS); or the Government Printing Office Monthly Catalog. A few others are produced at colleges and universities, such as DrugInfo, produced at the University of Minnesota.

The databases are then usually leased to the vendors, such as Dialog, BRS and SDC. The vendors charge the public for the right to access the databases and pay royalties to the producers. The vendors own the hardware and software used to access the databases. The software allows for the multiplicity of databases to be searched using standardized instructions or commands. Even so, each database has its own idiosyncracies, capabilities and limitations, all of which complicate database searching.

## ACCESS

The vendors allow the public to access their databases via telecommunications systems. It is necessary to have a keyboard and a terminal or microcomputer and a modem in order to connect to the vendor's mainframe computers, which could be located hundreds or thousands of miles away. A person who wants a computer-generated bibliography in many cases will contact a search intermediary, i.e., someone trained in the vendor's software system. The search intermediary is often a librarian, and computer search services are frequently based in libraries. However, there are many private, for-profit information companies that provide such services. Libraries generally provide computer-based searches more cheaply than private companies, but costs and follow-up services, such as delivering the documents, vary widely.

## SEARCH STRATEGY

After an information request is made and the needs are explained to the search intermediary, he or she must structure the request into a search strategy and decide which database or databases will contain the information being sought. The search intermediary determines appropriate key words or index terms to use, aided by thesauri that contain index terms.

Once the search strategy has been determined, the search intermediary dials into the telecommunication system, either through a long distance call or a telecommunications network. The latter is often less expensive than calling long distance.

The vendor assigns passwords to the search intermediary, who must use them in order to gain access to the computer banks. The appropriate database is asked for and, after the search intermediary signs on, the search strategy is typed into the computer. For example, the search intermediary may ask how many articles concerned with child abuse are contained in the database. The computer responds in a matter of seconds. It may tell you that there are 200. Since that is quite a few the requester may want to find out if alcoholism contributes to child abuse. The search intermediary then asks the computer how many articles on child abuse are also concerned with alcoholism. Since this defines a narrower aspect of the problem (two variables or index terms must be present instead of one), the number of retrievable citations should be smaller.

It is then possible to view the results, such as asking the computer to print the authors and titles of the articles so the search intermediary and requester can determine which ones are relevant. If the results are not relevant, the strategy can be changed. The ability to manipulate the search as it progresses is the interactive process usually referred to as online. Thus, searches can be narrowed or broadened, limited to particular years, certain authors, specific journals or languages.

Once it has been determined that the search strategy has produced the desired results, it is possible to print them, i.e., the bibliography and abstracts (not all bibliographic databases contain abstracts). The printing can be done while connected to the database (online printing) or after disconnecting, in which case it is sent through the mail (offline printing). The most cost-effective method for printing depends on the length of the bibliography, the hourly rate for the database, and the speed at which the local printer prints. It is usually less expensive to have the bibliography printed offline and mailed.

When finished, the search intermediary signs off, hangs up the telephone, and computes the cost of the search. Depending on the skills of the searcher, the speed at which the information can be received and printed and the complexity of the search and number of databases searched, the whole process may take no more than a half hour. It is possible to search a database containing over half a million bibliographic records spanning 20 years in only a few minutes or even seconds. To do the same thing manually using printed indexes could take hours or days.

## WHAT A SEARCH LOOKS LIKE*

Persons unfamiliar with computerized database searching are often in awe of the whole process. It sometimes appears as if the librarian is doing something magical during the computer search. It might be useful to have some familiarity with the appearance of a search prior to requesting one. Below is a sample search from the Social Work Abstracts database on the BRS search system.

ENTER DATABASE NAME _____ : swab
*SIGN ON   10:28:40   07/24/86
SWAB 1977 - MAY 1986
BRS SEARCH MODE - ENTER QUERY
  1__: child adj abuse
RESULT 299 DOCUMENTS
  2__: child-abuse.de.
RESULT 227 DOCUMENTS
  3__: child adj abuse.ti.
RESULT 117 DOCUMENTS
  4__: 2 and intervention.ti.
RESULT 6 DOCUMENTS
  5__: ..p 4 ti,de/1-6
  1

  TI  TITLE: Reducing child abuse through respite center intervention.
  DE  DESCRIPTOR/S: Child-abuse: respite program and reduction of. Battered-children. Respite-program: child abuse reduced through. Intervention: child abuse reduced by means of, provided at respite centers.
    2
  TI  TITLE: Characteristics of abused adolescents and guidelines for intervention.
  DE  DESCRIPTOR/S: Adolescents-Adolescence: abused, characteristics of, and guidelines for intervention. Child-abuse: adolescent and characteristics of victims of, and guidelines for intervention. Intervention: with abused adolescents, guidelines for.
    3
  TI  TITLE: The Family Support Center: early intervention for high-risk parents and children.
  DE  DESCRIPTOR/S: Intervention: early, with high-risk parents and children. Family-Support-Center: as early intervention for high-risk parents and children. Children: high-risk, early intervention for. Battered-children: Child-abuse: Family Support Center for preschool children at high risk. Child-neglect: Family Support Center for preschool children at high risk. Parents: high-risk, early intervention for.

END OF DOCUMENTS IN LIST
BRS SEARCH MODE - ENTER QUERY

---

*The sample searches that appear in this section were reprinted from the Social Work Abstract database and are used by permission of the National Association of Social Workers, Inc., Silver Spring, MD.

5__: ..p 4 all/3
3
AN  ACCESSION NUMBER: 9967. 853.
AU  AUTHOR/S: *Fraley-Y-L.
TI  TITLE: The Family Support Center: early intervention for high-risk parents and children
SO  SOURCE: Children Today, 12(1): 13-17, 1983.
AD  ADDRESS: *Family Support Center, Yeadon, Pa.
HC  HARDCOPY: 20(1):, 1984, No. 126.
DE  DESCRIPTOR/S: Intervention, early, with high-risk parents and children. Family-Support-Center: as early intervention for high-risk parents and children. Children: high-risk, early intervention for. Battered-children: Child-abuse: Family Support Center for preschool children at high risk. Child neglect: Family Support Center for preschool children at high risk. Parents: high-risk, early intervention for.
CC  CLASSIFICATION CODE: FAMILY-CHILD-WELFARE (CC2035).
PT  PUBLICATION TYPE: JOURNAL (J).
AB  ABSTRACT: The Family Support Center (FSC) in Yeadon, Pennsylvania, uses a multiphase, multidisciplinary approach to change the child-rearing patterns of parents and to remedy the developmental delays of preschool children at high-risk of being abused and neglected. Phase I of the program involves in-home counseling of parents. During Phase II, parents attend the Family School. The goals of this component of the program are (1) to provide a supportive environment in which parents are taught to create and maintain their own support systems, (2) to enhance parents' self-esteem through social encounters, shared responsibilities, nurturance, and experiential learning, (3) to help parents form more realistic expectations of their children's development, and (4) to teach basic parenting skills and provide nutrition education. Phase III involves three months of follow-up counseling. According to a three-year evaluation, the FSC's intervention strategy can reduce abuse and neglect, substantially minimize the need for costly out-of-home care, and help maintain and strengthen family life.

The sign-in time is given and then the label for the database (SWAB) and the years it covers (1977–May, 1986). The first request (child adj abuse) asks the computer to search for those two words adjacent to each other anywhere in the database. The result tells us that "child" adjacent to "abuse" appears in 299 documents. Since that is quite a few documents, the computer was told to find "child abuse" only where it is used as an index term or descriptor (DE), which resulted in 227 documents. Number 3 tells the computer to search for the "child" adjacent to "abuse" only in the titles of articles, which resulted in 117 documents. Since that is still quite a few documents, the computer was then told to go back to search statement 2 and look for "intervention" in the titles of the articles where "child abuse" was restricted to the index terms. The result was six documents. The computer was then told to print the titles and index terms for the six documents. Only the first three are reproduced in the illustration. Number 3 was chosen from the six documents and the full bibliographic record was printed.

Computer searches may also be done on authors' names. In order to find out if R. W. Toseland has articles indexed in Social Work Abstracts, his name was searched using the standard protocol. Seventeen documents authored by Toseland were found. The bibliographic citation for the first document was printed:

BRS SEARCH MODE - ENTER QUERY
5__: toseland-r.au.

RESULT 7 DOCUMENTS

BRS SEARCH MODE - ENTER QUERY
6__: ..p 6 bibl/1
1

  AN  ACCESSION NUMBER: 14243. 862.
  AU  AUTHOR/S *Toseland-R-W. Palmer-Ganeles-J. Chapman-D.
  TI  TITLE: Teamwork in psychiatric settings
  SO  SOURCE: Social Work, 31(1): 46-52, 1986.

The above examples show how quickly a database can be searched. The entire search took approximately seven minutes. The examples also illustrate the ease with which the search strategy and bibliography can be manipulated.

## ONLINE VERSUS PRINT

It is obvious that there are many advantages to retrieving bibliographic information electronically. Even though many of the databases exist in print form (many do not), there may be differences between the printed index and the electronic database. The database may be updated more frequently than the print version. Journal and/or document coverage may be broader in the online database.

Databases are more easily manipulated because they have many more access points than print indexes. The index in print form is generally accessed through an author index and a subject or keyword index. The subject or keyword index is limited to one term. But in databases each part of the bibliographic record is searchable. Journal names, institutional affiliations, publication years, and languages all serve as access points. And usually, but not always, several or more index terms are assigned to each record, enabling the searcher to look for a combination of terms, which helps to precisely focus the search.

The output of the search—the bibliography—can also be tailored to the needs of the requester. The bibliography can be sorted or arranged by author names, article titles, or titles of the journals, or they can be printed chronologically with the most recent materials printed first. Another key advantage to online searching is the ability to search for phrases that may be contained within the document title or abstract. This feature is particularly useful for retrieving articles or documents on new concepts or ideas for which there may not yet be an index term in either the print version or database.

To summarize, online databases present several advantages:

1. A very comprehensive bibliography can be produced from a variety of databases in a matter of minutes.
2. Literature can be retrieved that is so specific there may not be existing index terms.
3. New phases or concepts for which there may not be index terms can be searched.
4. The relationship of several subjects can be searched.
5. Online databases may be updated frequently, and new additions interfiled, eliminating the need to search year by year, volume by volume, as must be done when using printed indexes.
6. Frequent updates to a search can be produced. A search strategy can be stored in a computer and run against the database updates on a monthly

basis to retrieve new bibliographic additions without having to replicate an entire search each time.

7. Search strategies and resultant bibliographies can be tailored to individual needs.

There are also several disadvantages or caveats to online searching:

1. Online searches can be expensive, especially when several databases are searched or if the resultant bibliography is lengthy.
2. The requester must depend on the skills of the search intermediary. If the requester is not present during the search the results will depend solely on the skills and judgement of the searcher.
3. Search results depend on how well the search strategy was devised and the quality of indexing on the part of the database producer.
4. People often discover references when browsing through an index or the bookstacks in a library. Such discoveries may be tangential but still relevant or at least of interest but would have probably been missed in a precisely tailored computer search.
5. Persons who rely only on computer searches done through an intermediary may not learn how to find information for themselves if they have never used print sources.
6. Not all literature is indexed in online databases, and printed sources and card catalogs may still have to be manually searched. Many databases focus primarily on journal articles and exclude books or include only a few.
7. Older references may not be contained in a database, many of whose holdings date back only 5, 10, or 15 years.

## COSTS

Computer searches can be expensive. If a comprehensive literature search on a broad topic or topics for which there is a large quantity of literature is needed, the costs can be considerable. The costs also increase if several databases are searched and if the search strategy is lengthy, requiring more processing time. Databases vary in hourly rates and royalty charges.

Most searches are not prohibitively expensive. Although searches can run into hundreds of dollars, most cost no more than a new hardcover book or even as little as a paperback book. And the savings in time spent in the library are considerable.

## WHERE TO GET A SEARCH

Computer searches can be obtained at most medium- to large-sized libraries. Libraries were among the first organizations to offer access to commercial computerized databases. Private, for-profit information companies also provide such services, although usually at a higher cost. One advantage to using information companies is that they may be able to provide more services than a library can, such as providing the documents. A library may be able to do a computer search more inexpensively, but you may have to find the materials yourself.

Costs vary from one library or company to another. Private companies will add on charges to the basic costs to cover their additional expenses and to make a profit. Libraries often partially subsidize searches or at least do not charge for the time and training of the search intermediary. Some small libraries have formed consortiums to help defray costs; others rely on larger regional or state libraries to do the searches for them.

Many, if not most, college and university libraries offer computer-based literature searches. The public may be charged more than the university's own students and faculty, but it will probably still be cheaper than going through a private company. To find out about the availability of computer search services, call the nearest library and ask.

## DOING IT YOURSELF

In recent years many of the database vendors have begun providing database access to the home microcomputer market. People who have their own microcomputer and modem can, for a fee, obtain a password and dial up the database vendor themselves.

There are differences from the more traditional online services. Services aimed at the home microcomputer market provide access to databases through what is called a menu-driven system. After signing on to the system, the searcher is led through the search step-by-step by a series of questions. The computer asks the searcher what he or she wishes to do during each part of the search. In other words, the searcher selects options from a menu.

The more traditional or original approach to searching computer databases requires a familiarity with system protocols. The computer does not ask what you wish to do next. You must know what commands and steps to use. Searchers must be familiar with the system prior to signing on.

Both approaches have their advantages and disadvantages. The nonmenu-driven systems require prior training and a thorough familiarity with the search system and with the idiosyncracies of each database. It is important to have written documentation available to consult prior to or during the search. The original systems tend to be more comprehensive by providing access to all the databases offered by the vendor and the full range of search options.

The menu-driven systems, also referred to as user friendly, may offer a limited number of databases and search options. They also have somewhat less expensive hourly rates, but because it takes longer to go through each step, the final cost may not be much different. Because these systems are constantly evolving, check with the vendor to find out what the current costs are and what services are offered. All the major vendors—BRS, Dialog and SDC—have customer service departments, and their telephone numbers can be obtained by calling your local library.

## SOCIAL WORK AND SOCIAL WELFARE COVERAGE
## IN SOCIAL SCIENCE DATABASES

The primary database devoted to social work and social welfare is Social Work Abstracts, produced by the National Association of Social Workers. It closely corresponds to the print version *Social Work Research and Abstracts*, but its coverage only extends back to 1977 at present. The print version dates from 1965. Its inclusion in the BRS repertoire of databases was a welcome addition. Prior to its availability for online searching, there was no single database providing good coverage of social work journals.

Compared to some of the large social science databases, such as PsycInfo (*Psychological Abstracts*) and Sociological Abstracts, it contains a rather small number of bibliographic citations. Although there are over 12,000 citations in the database, it is dwarfed by the half million or more citations in PsycInfo and in Sociological Abstracts, both of which extend their coverage back to the mid–1960s. However, social work journals are not covered very comprehensively in the large social science databases, which greatly increases the importance of Social Work Abstracts to the social work community.

Social Work Abstracts primarily indexes journal articles, and descriptive abstracts are provided for most of the documents. Less than 10 percent of the citations are for doctoral dissertations in social welfare. A detailed review of Social Work Abstracts by this author appears in *DATABASE* 22, no. 1 (February 1986): 22–27.

Because of the small number of citations in Social Work Abstracts, other databases should be considered if good results are not obtained from SWAB or if a comprehensive bibliography is needed. There are a number of social science databases that provide coverage of social work journals and issues of interest to the social work community. Since many of the information needs of social workers pertain to therapies for psychological problems of clients, probably the most important is PsycInfo. Its large number of indexed articles and comprehensive journal coverage meets many informational needs. As previously noted, its spotty coverage of social work journals might also make a search of Social Work Abstracts necessary. Although a search of both databases may produce some overlap, they should be viewed as complementing each other.

A current version of PsycInfo and the medical database Medline is entitled Medical and Psychological Previews. It is produced by BRS as a current awareness service. It indexes core medical and psychological journals, and a few from related fields, as soon as they are received from the publisher. It is updated weekly and contains citations for the most current three months. PsycInfo is updated monthly.

A database produced by the National Institute of Mental Health entitled Mental Health Abstracts is also a good choice for a literature search. It is worldwide in scope and covers all types of mental health literature.

A spin-off from Sociological Abstracts, Social Welfare, Social Planning/Policy and Social Development: An International Database presents broad coverage of the applied social sciences including policy studies, welfare, administration, evaluation research, social work, health administration, and community organization.

Another possibility is Social SciSearch, the online version of *Social Sciences Citation Index*. It indexes the major journals in the social and behavioral sciences. It is interdisciplinary and presents a variety of viewpoints. The database is unique in that it allows for the retrieval of all papers that have either cited an earlier article or have been cited in a later article. Thus, research results can be traced forward and backward in time.

Social workers involved in school social work, or who work closely with those who are, might find the large and comprehensive database entitled ERIC quite useful. ERIC stands for Educational Resources Information Center, which is actually several information clearinghouses located in different cities around the United States. They collect and disseminate educational literature. Both journal articles and reports of all kinds are included.

## QUERY AS A GUIDE TO DATABASE SELECTION

All of the above-mentioned databases provide coverage of social work and psychological literature. The determining factor in selecting a database to search is the nature of the informational need or the question being asked. Discussing your needs with a trained searcher, usually a librarian, will help you decide which database to have searched.

The search in Social Work Abstracts on child abuse and intervention produced six article citations. If a similar search were run in PsycInfo the results would probably be much higher since it is a much larger database. A search of the database covering federal government publications would result in few citations concerning child abuse and intervention because clinical literature is not included. A search on child abuse might turn up congressional hearings and agency reports.

Whether you are requesting a computerized literature search by a trained searcher or are attempting to do it yourself, it would be useful to consult with an experienced searcher and to read whatever database documentation might be available.

Following is an alphabetical listing of pertinent social and behavioral databases. A few relevant nonsocial science databases are also included. Note: The databases are listed by their most common name.

## DATABASES

ABI Inform. 1971 to present. Indexes business journal literature covering most phases of management and administration including public sector issues. Producer: Data Courier. Availability: BRS, Dialog. Print equivalent: None.

ABLEDATA. Current. Provides information on rehabilitation products and technical aids for the disabled, including therapeutic, sensory, educational, vocational and transportation aids. Producer: National Rehabilitation Information Center, Catholic University of America. Availability: BRS. Print equivalent: None.

Alcohol Use and Abuse. 1968 to present. Includes information on treatment evaluation, chemical dependence, family therapy, the MMPI, and alcoholism among various populations. Producer: Drug Information Services, College of Pharmacy, University of Minnesota. Availability: BRS. Print equivalent: None.

American Statistics Index. 1973 to present. Provides a comprehensive listing of the statistical publications from most agencies of the U.S. government. For example, statistical publications of the Department of Health and Human Services are included. Producer: Congressional Information Service. Availability: Dialog. Print equivalent: *American Statistics Index.*

Catalyst Resources for Women. 1963 to present. Covers many diverse women's issues, especially those which relate to career and the corporate climate, such as two-career families, affirmative action, day care, working mothers, etc. Producer: Catalyst Library. Availability: BRS. Print equivalent: None.

Child Abuse and Neglect. 1965 to present. Indexes descriptions of ongoing research projects, audiovisual products, legal references, service programs and bibliographic references. Producer: National Center on Child Abuse and Neglect, Children's Bureau, U.S. Department of Health and Human Services. Availability: Dialog. Print equivalent: None.

Criminal Justice Periodical Index. 1975 to present. Indexes bulletins, digests and journals concerned with law enforcement and the administration of justice. Producer: University Microfilms. Availability: Dialog. Print equivalent: *Criminal Justice Periodical Index.*

DrugInfo. 1968 to present. Covers the educational, sociological and psychological aspects of alcohol and drug use and abuse. Producer: Drug Information Services, College of Pharmacy, University of Minnesota. Availability: BRS. Print equivalent: None.

Educational Resources Information Center. 1966 to present. Contains citations to research findings, project and technical reports, books and journal articles in education. Producers: National Institute of Education and ERIC Processing and Reference Facility. Availability: Dialog, BRS. Print equivalent: *Current Index to Journals in Education; Resources in Education.*

Embase. 1980 to present. Offers broad coverage of biomedicine and related biological sciences as well as health economics and administration, drug literature and toxicology. Producer: Elsevier Science Publishing. Availability: Dialog. Print equivalent: *Excerpta Medica.*

Family Resources. 1970 to present. Covers interdisciplinary literature related to family. Topics covered are marriage and divorce, family trends, organizations and services to families, family relationships, sexual attitudes and behavior, and therapy and education. Producer: National Council on Family Relations. Availability: Dialog, BRS. Print equivalent: None.

GPO Monthly Catalog. 1976 to present. Covers all public documents produced under the auspices of the U.S. government. Indexes publications of the legislative, judicial and executive branches. Producer: U.S. Government Printing Office. Availability: BRS, Dialog. Print equivalent: *Monthly Catalog of United States Government Publications.*

Health Planning and Administration. 1975 to present. Contains references to the nonclinical literature, including most aspects of health care planning, organization, financing, management, human resources, etc. Producer: National Library of Medicine. Availability: Dialog, BRS. Print equivalent: None.

Legal Resource Index. 1980 to present. Indexes law books, journals and newspaper articles on legal subjects. Producer: Information Access Company. Availability: Dialog, BRS. Print equivalent: *Legal Resource Index.*

Lexis. 1920s to present. Contains the entire text of most significant law cases. It includes cases from the U.S. Supreme Court, U.S. courts of appeals, U.S. district courts, regional and state courts. It also contains the United States Code. Producer: Mead Data Central. Availability: Libraries and law firms that subscribe to Lexis. Print equivalent: *United States Law Reports.*

Medical and Psychological Previews. Current three months. Indexes 160 core journals from medicine, psychology and related fields. It is updated weekly as compared to quarterly for many other databases. Producer: BRS. Availability: BRS. Print equivalent: None.

Medline. 1966 to present. Contains comprehensive listings of national and international medical literature. Producer: National Library of Medicine. Availability: Dialog, BRS. Print equivalent: *Index Medicus.*

Mental Health Abstracts. 1969 to present. Covers the international literature concerned with mental health. Producer: National Institute of Mental Health. Availability: Dialog. Print equivalent: None.

Mental Measurements Yearbook. 1977 to present. Contains factual information, critical reviews, and reliability-validity information on test materials, including tests of general achievement, intelligence, personality, speech and hearing, vocation and a wide range of subject specialties. Producer: Buros Institute of Mental Measurements, University of Nebraska, Lincoln. Availability: BRS. Print equivalent: *Mental Measurements Yearbook.*

National Criminal Justice Reference Service. 1972 to present. Irregularly updated. Indexes materials concerned with all aspects of law enforcement and criminal justice. Producer: National Criminal Justice Reference Service, National Institute of Justice. Availability: Dialog. Print equivalent: *NCJRS Microfiche Collection.*

National Technical Information Service. 1964 to present. Indexes all U.S. government-sponsored research reports and studies in all subjects, including the behavioral and social sciences. Surprisingly good coverage of social welfare materials. Producer: National Technical Information Service, U.S. Department of Commerce. Availability: Dialog, BRS. Print equivalent: *Government Reports Announcements and Index.*

PAIS International. 1972 to present. Covers social and public policy literature, including public administration, social welfare and law. Also selectively indexes U.S. government publications. Producer: Public Affairs Information Service. Availability: Dialog, BRS. Print equivalent: *Public Affairs Information Service Bulletin.*

REHABDATA. 1950 to present. Provides access to documents and audiovisuals focusing on various aspects of rehabilitation of the physically or mentally disabled. Producer: National Rehabilitation Information Center, Catholic University of America. Availability: BRS. Print equivalent: None.

SciSearch. 1974 to present. Covers, as a multidisciplinary database, the most significant science and technology journals. Producer: Institute for Scientific Information. Availability: Dialog, BRS. Print equivalent: *Science Citation Index.*

Social SciSearch. 1972 to present. Covers, as a multidisciplinary database, the most significant social science journals as well as many books. This database, like SciSearch, includes references and bibliographies from the indexed articles that show who was cited by an author. Producer: Institute for Scientific Information. Availability: Dialog, BRS. Print equivalent: *Social Sciences Citation Index.*

Social Welfare, Social Planning/Policy and Social Development: An International Database. 1979 to present. Presents broad coverage of the applied social science literature, including policy studies, welfare administration, evaluation research, social work, health administration, and community organization. Producer: Sociological Abstracts. Availability: Dialog, BRS. Print equivalent: *Social Welfare, Social Planning/Policy and Social Development: An International Database.*

Social Work Abstracts. 1977 to present. Indexes articles from most social work and social welfare journals. Also includes abstracts of social work doctoral dissertations. Producer: National Association of Social Workers. Availability: BRS. Print equivalent: *Social Work Research and Abstracts.*

Sociological Abstracts. 1963 to present. Covers worldwide sociology literature and related disciplines, such as family studies, gerontology, policy sciences, etc. Producer: American Sociological Association. Availability: Dialog, BRS. Print equivalent: *Sociological Abstracts.*

Westlaw. 1920s to present. Contains the entire text of most significant law cases. It includes cases from the U.S. Supreme Court, U.S. courts of appeals, U.S. district courts, and regional and state courts. It also contains the United States Code and Code of Federal Regulations. Producer: West Publishing Company. Availability: Libraries and law firms that subscribe to Westlaw. Print equivalent: West's *National Reporter System.*

# CHAPTER 6
# Books

Scholarly books are generally narrowly focused on specific subjects and are frequently referred to as monographs. Technically, monographs are an intermediate form of publication that tend to be longer than journal articles but shorter than most books. They are published as a separate physical entity. Many times they are part of a series of related works, for example, a monographic series on the psychology of aging in which each separate book is devoted to an aspect of the psychology of aging. In practice the terms "book" and "monograph" are often used synonymously.

In the literature of social work, as in most social and behavioral sciences, books and journal articles are both used for reporting original research. In the natural sciences far more original research is published in journal articles while books play a secondary role, almost always summarizing and interpreting previously reported research.

In the social and behavioral sciences the distinction between books and journal articles is not always so clear. Journal articles are narrowly focused while books that report original research are likely to be wider in scope and have greater detail. In addition to reporting research, books may also attempt to summarize and synthesize the research with what is already known. New ideas usually first appear in journal articles. A new theory or study is likely to be narrowly focused and reported in a journal. It may be followed by more journal articles by the same author or by other authors that investigate other aspects of the problem or attempt to support or refute the first study. Research that is controversial, regardless of whether it is good or bad, will spawn more research. Once a new area of inquiry has grown and become established, books appear that summarize, synthesize and interpret. Textbooks are examples of books that do the latter. Ideas in textbooks are often presented as established truths, but many of these "established truths" are still being debated in academic circles.

Another consideration in using books is the time factor. It generally takes longer to write a book than it does a journal article. It also takes time to prepare a book for publication and to distribute it to bookstores and libraries. It is necessary to advertise books, and it takes time for interested scholars to read and review them and to determine their quality and usefulness. The contents of books are not always subjected to the same scholarly scrutiny while being prepared as are journal articles. The system of peer review for journal articles is explained in Chapter 4, "Social Work and Related Journals."

Journal articles may be the preeminent type of literature in the social and behavioral sciences, but books run a close second, especially in social work. Social work practice methods and techniques are often published in book form. Numerous how-to books describing methods and techniques for all sorts of therapies can be found in a social work library.

Thus, books are an important format within the social work literature. Besides reporting research and serving as texts, books, as noted, may contain collections of essays, present overviews and new developments within a field, as well as present bibliographies. (See the section on handbooks in Chapter 2, "Brief Information: Reference Books.")

## CARD CATALOGS

Libraries use card catalogs (sometimes called public catalogs) for listing their books. Card catalogs consist of alphabetized files of cards listing a library's books by author, title and subject. The author, title and subject cards may be interfiled in one catalog or may be divided into separate catalogs. When using a card catalog it is a good idea to know how it is arranged and in which part of it you are looking. It is surprising how many people will look for subject cards among the title cards and vice versa.

Authors are listed by their last names; authors who write under pseudonyms may have their books listed under their real name and their pseudonym listed on a card with a "see" reference to their real name. Libraries differ on such practices, so rather than getting frustrated when using a card catalog, ask a librarian for help.

Sometimes authors may be more than a single person, that is, an organization, society, institution or government agency. These are called corporate authors. If you are looking for corporate authors it is essential to know the correct name. Editors of books are usually, but not always, listed in card catalogs. Books with two or more authors may have cards filed under both names. In library parlance the author or authors of a book are referred to as main entries. If there is no author, the title card is the main entry. The main entry cards generally provide the most complete information on a book. The additional cards may be less thorough.

If you do not know the author you can look under the title of the book. You do need to know the exact title. When filing title cards librarians ignore the initial article "a," "an" or "the" in the title and file under the next word.

Looking for books by subject is how most people begin a literature search. The main trick is to know which subject to look under. Card catalog subject headings may not be what you expect them to be. For example, books on child abuse may be found under "Child Abuse," but they may also be listed under "Abused Children," "Child Welfare" and "Child Molesting." Libraries often provide cross-references that refer you to selected subjects. If you have found a useful book under author or title, look at the notes at the bottom of the card (called tracings) to discover what subjects it is listed under in order to look up related books.

The best way to find out which subjects to look under is to use the list of subject headings that all libraries provide. If a library uses the Library of Congress system for organizing its books it will have the *Library of Congress Subject Headings* in two volumes. Make sure you are using the latest edition, currently the tenth. In addition to providing the correct subject headings it also presents cross-references and terms not used. In other words, you may have assumed a subject would be listed but the *LC Subject Headings* will tell you that the card catalog does not use that particular term to list books under. If a library uses the Dewey Decimal system you may find that it uses the *Sears List of Subject Headings*. The *Sears List* is mostly used in smaller public and school libraries.

Subject headings can also be used to find reference books, such as dictionaries, encyclopedias and bibliographies. Book-length bibliographies will be listed under the subject followed by a dash and then "Bibliography," e.g. "Drug Abuse—Bibliography." Dictionaries, encyclopedias, handbooks and journals are listed the same way.

## ONLINE CATALOGS

Many libraries are now using or planning to use online catalogs. Online catalogs are computerized databases that contain, in theory, all the information in a card catalog. In practice, online catalogs vary greatly. Some are better than others. Some contain all the information card catalogs do, while others provide less. Some can be searched only by author, title or subject, while others can be searched by combinations of authors and titles or key words in titles. Some online catalogs are really only automated circulation systems. Many libraries provide public access terminals for their circulation systems, so keep in mind that the information such systems can provide is usually not as complete as that found in a fully developed online catalog. Most libraries are largely limited in developing online catalogs by the amount of money they have to spend. Developing an online catalog is expensive and takes time. However, it is the direction in which many libraries are going. When using an online catalog or automated circulation system for the first time, consult with a librarian or at least read the instructions.

## CALL NUMBERS

In the upper left hand corner of a card catalog card or somewhere on the terminal screen of an online catalog is the call number. Call numbers represent classification schemes libraries use to organize their books. They show the location or address of a book on the library's shelves. Most medium to large libraries employ one of two classification schemes: the Dewey Decimal Classification System or the Library of Congress Classification System. Most large libraries now use the LC system or are in the process of switching from Dewey to LC. Still others may have once used Dewey, switched to LC, and yet never bothered to change the older books, resulting in a split system. If you are using a large library it is a good idea to check and see which classification system the library uses.

The Dewey system is numeric while LC is alphanumeric. Major categories of the Dewey Decimal Classification System are as follows:

| | |
|---|---|
| 000-099: General Works | 500-599: Pure Science |
| 100-199: Philosophy | 600-699: Technology |
| 200-299: Religion | 700-799: The Arts |
| 300-399: Social Sciences | 800-899: Literature |
| 400-499: Language | 900-999: History |

Categories in the Library of Congress Classification System are as follows:

| | |
|---|---|
| A: | General Works/Polygraphy |
| B: | Philosophy/Religion |
| C: | History/Auxiliary Sciences |
| D: | History and Topography (except America) |
| E/F: | America |
| G: | Geography |
| H: | Social Sciences |
| J: | Political Science |
| K: | Law |
| L: | Education |
| M: | Music |
| N: | Fine Arts |
| P: | Language and Literature |

Q:  Science
R:  Medicine
S:  Agriculture/Plant and Animal
T:  Technology
U:  Military Science
V:  Naval Science
Z:  Bibliography and Library Science

Most social work and social welfare books fall into the HV class. So do criminal justice materials. H is the class for the social sciences, and the second letter denotes a subclass. Sociology falls into the HM class. Psychology books may be found in the BFs, psychiatry in the RCs and medicine in the other R classes. The method of classifying books is somewhat arbitrary, and books that seem like they should be next to each other on the shelves often are not. This is one important reason for using the subject catalog, which groups books by subjects and related subjects rather than by call number.

## OCLC AND RLIN

There are presently two large nationwide online databases that contain the bibliographic records for millions of books: OCLC and RLIN. Technically, they are bibliographic databases.

When library staff acquires a new book they may catalog it and classify it themselves, or they may first search OCLC or RLIN to see if another library has already cataloged it, and if so, how. Many librarians look for books that have been cataloged by the Library of Congress. If there is an LC record it is usually copied. In fact, librarians in libraries that use OCLC or RLIN merely need push a key on their terminal and the catalog cards are produced at OCLC or RLIN and mailed to the library.

OCLC is the larger of the two systems, and many different types of libraries across the United States and in foreign countries participate in it. RLIN is the database for the Research Libraries Group, which consists mostly of large research libraries. Many libraries provide public access terminals and instructions for using OCLC or RLIN. In addition to providing the same bibliographic information as do card catalogs, the two databases can indicate which library actually owns a book. If the library you are using does not own a book, it is not difficult to find out which does. If there are no public access terminals, many libraries will search OCLC or RLIN for you. They are powerful tools for finding books and should not be overlooked.

## INTERLIBRARY LOAN

The library may not have the book you want. All libraries are limited in the number of books and journals they can afford to buy. Another problem is that books go out of print quickly. "Out of print" means that the publisher of the book has sold all of the copies of the book and does not plan to print additional copies. Library books are frequently stolen or mutilated and, if out of print, cannot easily be replaced.

If the library you are using does not have the book you need, it will try to borrow it for you from another library. This service is called interlibrary loan. The same is true for journal articles. Fees for interlibrary loan may vary. The service is sometimes provided free of charge. It does, however, take time, which is a good reason for not waiting until the last minute to begin library research.

## BOOK REVIEWS

Finding book reviews is not difficult. Many, if not most, scholarly journals publish book reviews. Books take time to be reviewed. Book reviews often do not appear until a year or more after a book has been published. A few journals publish their own indexes which include book reviews, but most do not.

The quickest way to locate book reviews is to use a book review index or a journal index that indexes book reviews. Examples of the former are *Book Review Digest* and *Book Review Index*. The *Book Review Digest* focuses on popular books and, in addition to summarizing the reviews, tells you where the full review appears. The *Book Review Index* covers book reviews of social science books. Another source is the *Social Sciences Index*, which contains a separate section in each issue that indexes book reviews. The *Education Index* and the *Index to Legal Periodicals* contain a similar feature for reviews of books in their subjects. Many of the other indexing and abstracting services described in Chapter 3, "Journal and Newspaper Articles," also index book reviews.

## CONCLUSION

Books contain a cornucopia of information on many social work and related topics. Books can present original research, summarize and synthesize a subject and present factual reference material. When researching a subject keep in mind that books are not the only sources and may in fact not be the best sources for current information. It is important to know how the library you are using organizes and provides access to its books. Computer data storage is increasingly becoming the primary means for keeping track of books. And it is important to remember that if one library does not have a book it can usually borrow it from another library.

## SOURCES DISCUSSED

### Card Catalogs

*Library of Congress Subject Headings.* 10th edition. Washington, DC: Library of Congress, 1986.
Westby, Barbara M., editor. *Sears List of Subject Headings.* New York: H. W. Wilson, 1972.

### Books Reviews

*Book Review Digest.* New York: H. W. Wilson, 1905 to present.
*Book Review Index.* Detroit, Michigan: Gale Research, 1965 to present.
*Education Index.* New York: H. W. Wilson, 1929 to present.
*Index to Legal Periodicals.* New York: H. W. Wilson, 1908 to present.

# CHAPTER 7
# Public Documents

Publications from the federal government and from state and local governments represent an important source of information for social workers and other persons involved in human services. Defining public documents is difficult since such documents take many forms. They may be printed documents or publications or may be a microform, an audiovisual or a machine-readable data file. Government publications are generally produced wholly or partially at government expense. Many federal government publications are not in the public domain but are classified with dissemination restricted. However, many if not most government publications are available to the public, and it is the publicly available material that this chapter will focus on.

This chapter discusses the various types of government publications, their usefulness for the human services and how to access them. It also presents secondary or nongovernmental sources of information on government. The primary emphasis is on U.S. federal government publications, but state and local publications are included. Chapter 8, "Statistics" also presents many government publications and sources. Some repetition is unavoidable, but the two chapters complement each other.

In addition to identifying and describing government publications, this chapter also illustrates how libraries organize documents and make them available to the public. Material included in this chapter is selective and by no means comprehensive.

## FEDERAL PUBLICATIONS

The United States federal government is the largest publisher of information in the world. Hundreds of thousands of documents of all sorts emanate from the federal government every year. Much of it is poorly controlled and difficult to access, and access and use are becoming even more difficult due to recent fiscal retrenchment policies. In the early 1980s governmental review of publishing practices resulted in the elimination of 2,000 publications. Some of the eliminated material was no doubt ephemeral, but many important and useful programs were also cut.

In addition, much information previously published in paper format changed to microfiche and computer tape. Such cost-saving measures make it more difficult for the general public to be informed. As Morehead points out in his *Introduction to United States Public Documents,* "What began as a program to eliminate trivial and duplicative films, periodicals, and pamphlets has been transformed into a systematic assault on access to public information" (p. 28). Nevertheless, the federal government continues to produce an avalanche of information, much of which is useful to social workers.

## Government Printing Office

The Government Printing Office (GPO) is part of Congress (the legislative branch) and does much of the publishing, printing and binding for the federal government. Many federal documents are not GPO publications, being published in-house at departments and agencies. The GPO also contracts with commercial publishers for the printing of many documents. Whether commercially produced through a contractual agreement or printed at the GPO, a GPO document will bear the imprint "U.S. Government Printing Office."

## Superintendent of Documents

The Office of the Superintendent of Documents within the GPO serves several important functions. The Superintendent of Documents sells to the public government publications produced by or through the GPO, compiles and publishes catalogs and indexes of government publications, distributes government publications to designated libraries that serve as depositories, and mails some government publications for members of Congress and government agencies.

Many libraries organize their collections of federal government documents according to a system devised by the Superintendent of Documents called the SuDocs Classification System. The letters and numbers in parentheses following each title in this chapter are the SuDocs numbers. The SuDocs System is described more fully below.

Individuals may purchase many public documents at reasonable cost from the Superintendent of Documents. The GPO maintains bookstores in several large cities. A current list of bookstores with addresses and phone numbers can be found in the *Monthly Catalog of United States Government Publications,* described later in this chapter. Some government publications can also be found in commercial bookstores. GPO publications are not copyrighted and are often reproduced by commercial publishers, usually at higher prices than the government charges.

## Depository Library System

Fortunately it is not necessary to purchase most government documents. The Superintendent of Documents, as noted, maintains a mailing program to libraries across the country. The current general depository system exists in two parts: regional depositories and selective depositories.

There are over 50 regional depository libraries across the U.S. Regional depositories are supplied with both paper copy and microfiche of GPO publications. Regional depositories receive at least one copy of all available depository items and make them available to the public. Most, but not all, states have a regional depository, which may be the official state library or the library of a major university. Regional depositories must make their documents available to other libraries in their region, often through interlibrary loan.

Selective depositories, of which there are more than 1,300, may choose from the myriad federal publications. Usually they choose materials that meet the needs of their clientele. Many libraries located near each other cooperate in purchasing federal documents to help save money and space. A university that has human service programs will probably acquire most publications from the Department of Health and Human Services.

## Finding Government Documents in the Library

Federal publications are usually housed as a separate collection in most libraries. Because of the volume of documents they are seldom cataloged and entered into the card catalog or online catalog. Most federal documents are organized according to the Superintendent of Documents Classification System, referred to as SuDocs. It is an alphanumeric system based on the principle of provenance: the several publications of any government department, bureau, agency, office, etc. are grouped together under like notation. It is not a subject arrangement but rather reflects the organization of the federal government. Provenance does not particularly show authorship, only who or which agency had an item printed.

When the federal government reorganizes a frequent occurrence, so does the SuDocs system. A recurring publication, such as the *Budget of the United States Government,* may be found in several different locations with several different SuDocs classes. This is frustrating to both librarians and persons seeking the documents. It might be best to ask a librarian for help in locating federal documents.

A brief example of the SuDocs system might help. Letters are used to indicate the parent agency. For example, Ju is used for the judiciary, Pr Ex for the President, and He for the Department of Health and Human Services. Subordinate bureaus and offices are denoted by numbers, followed by decimals to note the type of publication, e.g., annual report, law, press release, handbook, etc. Additional letters and numbers may reflect authorship, edition and year of publication. Although it can get a little more complicated, that is the basic system.

SuDocs numbers have been listed after the above-described federal publications. Item number refers to a control number for a publication that remains constant even if the title or issuing agency changes. It can be useful for ordering documents.

## Catalogs and Indexes

### Books

The Superintendent of Documents publishes several current awareness bibliographic tools that identify federal government publications. *U.S. Government Books* (G.P. 3.17/5; item 556-A) is a quarterly current awareness ordering tool. It contains approximately 1,000 annotations for popular books and serial publications that can be purchased from the Office of the Superintendent of Documents. Order forms are provided in each issue. A more current publication is the bimonthly *New Books* (G.P. 3.1716; item 556-B), an annotated listing of all new titles placed on sale during the preceding two months.

### Periodicals

Recurring or serial publications are listed in a quarterly called Price List 36 (G.P. 3.9; item 554). It is an annotated bibliography of over 500 recurring publications. Recurring publications are dated periodicals and publications that consist of a basic volume updated by changes or new material issued for a predetermined or indefinite period. This includes many of the serial statistical publications, such as the *Social Security Bulletin* described in the following chapter. There is no subject index, but there is a detailed agency index. Order forms are included.

There are two commercially published indexes to U.S. government periodicals. They may be easier to use than *Price List 36* or the *Monthly Catalog.* The *Index to Government Periodicals* is a quarterly that indexes about 150 selected U.S. government periodicals. *The Guide to United States Government Serials and Periodicals* is an annual publication that indexes serials, periodicals and irregular publications of the federal government. It is arranged alphabetically by branch of government, department and agency. Agency, subject and title indexes are provided.

## Subject Bibliographies

The federal government publishes numerous *Subject Bibliographies* on a wide range of subjects, including many social welfare topics. They are arranged alphabetically by title, and many of the entries are annotated. Ordering information is provided. An index to this series is the *Subject Bibliography Index*. One can order either the series or the index or both, but the index and the bibliographies will be in most regional and selective depository libraries.

## General Sources

One of the most widely used current awareness tools is the *GPO Sales Publications Reference File* (G.P. 3.3312; item 552-B). It is a microfiche catalog of all currently available publications from the Superintendent of Documents. It also lists forthcoming and out-of-stock titles. At any one time it may list about 25,000 titles. It is issued bimonthly and also exists as a database available through Dialog Information Systems. There is also a monthly entitled *GPO New Sales Publications,* which lists forthcoming publications, new publications and reprints. Price and ordering information are provided.

Perhaps the most widely known bibliography is the *Monthly Catalog of United States Government Publications* (G.P. 3.8; item 557). It lists publications issued by all branches of the federal government and contains about 27,000 entries per year. The entries are grouped alphabetically by agency, with the monthly indexes cumulated semiannually and annually. It uses Library of Congress subject headings and provides full bibliographic details for each item but does not include annotations. There are author, title, subject and series/reports number indexes. The bibliographic information also includes the SuDocs classification number for each item, which allows you to find the document in libraries that use the SuDocs numbers for arranging the documents on their shelves.

Most libraries of any size will have the *Monthly Catalog.* It is a basic reference tool. Because many libraries do not catalog federal government publications and do not list them in their card catalogs or online catalogs, the *Monthly Catalog* often serves as the primary tool for locating government documents. It also is available in database form from all major database vendors.

## Statistics

The bibliographic tools described above contain all types of federal publications, including publications containing statistical information. Because bibliographies like the *Monthly Catalog* are so voluminous, it is time-consuming to wade through them to locate sources of statistical information. One index that serves as an aid for finding statistical information is the commercially produced *American Statistics Index.* It attempts to be a master guide and index to all the statistical publications of the U.S. government. *American Statistics Index* and many of the statistical publications it indexes and abstracts are described in the following chapter.

## Technical Reports

The federal government sponsors millions of dollars of research in many fields of inquiry. Some, but not all of it, is published by the GPO. The National Technical Information Service (NTIS) was created to improve access to data files and scientific and technical reports produced by federal agencies and their contractors. It is the central source for the public sale of U.S. government-sponsored research. Much of the research is oriented toward engineering and science, but there is an abundance of behavioral and social science research, much of it relevant for social work. Because much of the technical report literature is not disseminated through the depository system, NTIS serves as a clearinghouse and sales service for such literature and does include some GPO items.

Many large libraries collect NTIS documents. They can also be purchased from NTIS. The basic index for identifying NTIS documents is the *Government Reports Announcements and Index.* It is an indexing and abstracting service containing current citations of all publications received by NTIS. It is semimonthly and is cumulated in the *Government Reports Annual Index.* Both have key word, personal author, corporate author, contract/grant number and NTIS report number indexes. A separate microfiche title index is called the *NTIS Title Index.* NTIS also exists as a database available through all the major database vendors.

## Reference Sources and Directories

A basic reference source on the federal government found in most libraries is the *United States Government Manual.* An annual publication from the GPO, it describes the programs and activities of the legislative, judicial and executive branches. Its organizational charts and descriptions of programs and activities are useful for social workers dealing with the federal establishment. It is indexed by name, subject and agency.

There are several commercial sources that complement the *U.S. Government Manual.* Whitnah's *Government Agencies* is an encyclopedia describing the history, administrative structure, failures, achievements and conflicts of over 100 U.S. government organizations. The *Federal Regulatory Directory* is a biennial guide to regulatory agencies. It includes information on their history, power and authority, background of commissioners and/or members, organization, information sources and references. There is also an introduction to the topic of regulation.

A companion volume is the *Washington Information Directory,* an annual that provides information on agencies of the executive branch, Congress, and nongovernmental organizations in the Washington, DC, area. It includes the name, address and phone number for each organization, name and title of the director or contact person, and a description of the work performed. It is arranged by 16 subject areas and has organizational name and subject indexes.

The *Federal Yellow Book* is a loose-leaf service, updated bimonthly, that provides directory information for about 27,000 federal employees by organization, with names, titles, addresses, locations and phone numbers.

The *Federal Executive Directory* provides an alphabetical index to federal executive names and a key-word index to agency names. The *Federal Staff Directory* provides biographical and directory information on key staff in the executive branch.

The *Encyclopedia of Governmental Advisory Organizations* serves as a guide to approximately 5,000 permanent, continuing and ad hoc U.S. presidential advisory commissions, Congressional advisory commissions, task forces, etc. It includes name, address and phone numbers, officials, history and authority, programs, recommendations, members, staff, publications and meetings. It is arranged in 10 general subject sections and has key-word, name, subject, publications, reports, presidential administration and agency indexes.

## Congressional Information

Congress is the branch of the federal government that enacts the laws of the United States, including the legislation that governs the welfare state. Thus, it is of interest to social workers to have some idea of how to identify and find congressional publications and to trace public legislation.

A widely used commercial source from Commerce Clearing House for current information on Congress is the *Congressional Index*. It is a rather complex index organized by divisions. There are subject and author indexes and a separate index entitled "Headline Legislation," which covers bills that have received widespread media attention. "House Bills," "House Resolutions," "Senate Bills" and "Senate Resolutions" list date of introduction and number and include a descriptive title, name of author or original sponsors, a summary of the legislative provisions and the committee to which it was referred. "Status of House Bills" reports House measures from the time hearings are held on them to final enactment or rejection. Within these divisions are current status tables which update the main listings as the session progresses. "Enactment-Vetoes" lists new laws. It is arranged by public law number, original bill number, subject and author. If a bill was vetoed by the President, this section lists the bill and notes whether Congress overrode the veto.

The Library of Congress' Congressional Research Service publishes the *Digest of Public General Bills and Resolutions* (LC 14.6; item 807), which provides summaries of the main provisions of public bills and resolutions during the legislative process.

The *Congressional Record* is the official proceedings of Congress. It consists of four parts: "Proceedings of the House," "Proceedings of the Senate," "Extensions of Remarks" and "Daily Digest." The biweekly index to the *Congressional Record* has a section called "History of Bills and Resolutions." It provides legislative status information from a bill's introduction to enactment or veto. Dialog Information Services has a database entitled Congressional Records Abstracts, which provides comprehensive abstracts covering each issue of the *Congressional Record.*

A commercial publishing company, Congressional Information Service, publishes the *CIS Index to Publications of the United States Congress.* It attempts comprehensive indexing and abstracting of current congressional documents (except bills). It is arranged by committee and subdivided by type of publication, e.g., documents, hearings, reports, etc., It gives bibliographic data, availability and brief abstracts describing the item's content. The indexes are by subject, name, title, bill, report and document number, and committee and subcommittee chairpersons. It is a monthly and is cumulated annually. The annual cumulation of the document abstracts includes an important comparison volume, *CIS Legislative History Service,* which provides legislative histories.

Legislative histories provide a summary of testimony, reports, etc., that indicate the history and intent of new laws. In addition to the CIS publication, another source that provides legislative histories as well as the text of public laws is the *United States Code Congressional and Administrative News.*

Two useful and widely known publications concerned with Congress are published by the Congressional Quarterly Service. *Congressional Quarterly Weekly Report* is a current awareness service which contains detailed coverage of Congress, the presidency, the Supreme Court and national politics. It provides discussions of major legislation, presidential legislative requests, etc.

The *Congressional Quarterly Almanac* is a hardbound volume published after each congressional session. It is a summary of the congressional session. CQS also publishes the *Congressional Roll Call,* which provides a complete voting record of every member of Congress on every item.

The *Official Congressional Directory* (Y4.P93/1:1; item 992) contains current biographical information on each member of Congress. This annual publication also contains information on committees and subcommittees and statistical data on Congress. The *Congressional Staff Directory* is an annual publication which focuses on the staffs of the congressional members and on the staffs of the congressional committees and subcommittees. Finally, the *Congressional Yellow Book* is a loose-leaf service that provides directory information on senators and representatives, their office and committee staffs, state delegations and district offices.

## Federal Laws

Once Congress enacts new laws and they are signed into law by the President they are sent to libraries as slip laws. Slip laws are individual copies of the law. They are compiled into the *United States Statutes at Large,* a chronological arrangement of new laws. Eventually all public law is codified in the *United States Code,* which contains a subject index. Chapter 9, "The Law," discusses legal research.

## Presidential Publications

The Office of the Presidency publishes several important publications. A well-known publication is the *Federal Register* (GS 4.107). The *Federal Register* is published daily, Monday through Friday, and consists of the rules, proposed rules and notices put out by the executive departments, agencies and independent utilities. Presidential documents such as Executive Orders and Proclamations are also published in the *Federal Register.* The index to the *Federal Register* is called, appropriately enough, the *Federal Register Index.*

The President must execute the laws enacted by Congress. Congress delegates to the departments and agencies within the executive branch the power to issue rules and regulations that have the force of law. As noted, these rules and regulations first appear in the *Federal Register.* Eventually they are compiled in the *Code of Federal Regulations (CFR).* The CFR is divided into 50 sections or titles and is revised once a year. There is an index called the *CFR Index.* Using the *CFR Index* is the best way to tap into the myriad federal rules and regulations which govern many aspects of modern life.

Thus, new laws are compiled in *United States Statutes at Large* and eventually the *United States Code.* Rules and regulations flow from the *Code* and are first published in the *Federal Register.* They are compiled annually in the *Code of Federal Regulations.* The previously mentioned *Federal Regulatory Directory* serves as a guide to the regulatory agencies.

## United States Budget

One of the most important presidential documents is the *Budget of the United States Government* (Pr Ex 2.8; item 853). It contains the budget message of the President and provides an overview of his budget proposals. Spending programs are explained in terms of national needs, agencies, missions, tax programs, etc. There is an *Appendix* (Pr Ex 2.8/App; item 853), which contains more detailed data on appropriations and funds. A less technical edition designed for use by the general public is the *United States Budget in Brief* (Pr Ex 2.8/2; item 855-A). A supplementary report, *Major Themes and Additional Budget Details* (Pr Ex 2.8/themes; item 853), describes budget implementation and the effects of specific programmatic changes.

A related publication useful to social workers is the *Catalog of Federal Domestic Assistance* (Pr Ex 2.20; item 853-A-1). The *Catalog* presents information on federal assistance programs. Program descriptions are indexed by department and agency names, applicant eligibility, functional classification, subject, popular names, and deadlines.

## STATE AND LOCAL PUBLICATIONS

Publications of state and local governments and municipalities are not subjected to the same degree of bibliographic control as are federal publications. Although state and local governments generate a large volume of materials, they do not always attempt to disseminate them in a manner that would allow publishers and libraries to acquire, organize, classify and make the documents available to others. Thus, it is more difficult for the public to access state and local publications. Fortunately, there are a couple of bibliographic control tools that make the job easier. They may not be comprehensive in coverage, but without them it would be much more difficult to find out what state and local governments publish.

Official state libraries are often the best places to find state publications. State departments and agencies are generally required to submit their publications to the state library, but compliance is often haphazard. State and local publications may be cataloged as books and be made available through the card catalog or online catalog, or they may be classified by a system other than Dewey Decimal or Library of Congress. It is necessary to check with the library you are using to find out how state and local documents are organized.

### Monthly Checklist

The primary indexing tool for state documents is produced by the Library of Congress. It is the *Monthly Checklist of State Publications* and is published by the GPO. The Library of Congress acquires more than 19,000 state documents annually. The *Monthly Checklist* is an alphabetical arrangement by state, territory or possession. Special sections cover publications of associations of state officials and regional organizations, state library surveys, studies, manuals and statistical reports. Full bibliographic information for each document is provided. There is an annual index.

### Red and Blue Books

Most state governments publish an annual manual. These manuals are usually referred to as red books or blue books. They are basic information sources on state governments and may include descriptions of departments and agencies and biographies of elected and key appointed officials. Sources of statistical information on state and local governments are presented in the following chapter.

## URBAN DOCUMENTS

Publications of municipal and county governments and organizations are a rich source of information but even more difficult to identify and obtain than state publications. Local governments do not always send copies of their publications to the local library or otherwise make them available to the public. The best identification tool is a commercially produced index, the *Index to Current Urban Documents*. It represents a systematic effort to identify local government publications. Documents are listed geographically by state and city or county, then by government agency. Brief annotations are usually provided for the documents. There is a detailed subject index. Greenwood Press, the publisher of this index, actually acquires the documents and places them on microfiche. These microfiche are called the *Urban Documents Microfiche Collection*. Documents can be individually ordered from Greenwood, or subscriptions can be set up for part or all of the collection. Many larger libraries will subscribe to parts of the collection, such as the documents from their local area. This is published quarterly with a cumulated annual volume.

## FOREIGN DOCUMENTS

British publications are often of interest to social work students and educators. The British equivalent of the *Monthly Catalog* is the *Catalogue of Government Publications*. It is a monthly listing of parliamentary and nonparliamentary publications from Her Majesty's Stationery Office, similar to the U.S. Government Printing Office.

United Nations publications are indexed in *UNDOC: Current Index*. This is the major index to UN publications and is published monthly except for July and August. It is arranged by agency and has subject, author, and title indexes. It is cumulated annually.

Larger college and university libraries and large public libraries usually acquire many British and UN publications. Once again, they may or may not be cataloged with the books, so it is best to ask for assistance in locating such publications.

## CONCLUSION

Publications of all levels of government are of value to social workers, social work students, educators, policymakers and other human service personnel. Because they are somewhat more difficult to obtain than books and journal articles they are often overlooked as informational sources.

However, once you have become familiar with the basic governmental information sources and bibliographic finding aids, the task of locating government publications becomes easier. Many libraries employ librarians who specialize in document librarianship. These persons are valuable resources and will be able to help steer you through the maze of government publications.

## SOURCES DISCUSSED

### Catalogs and Indexes

#### *Books*

United States. Superintendent of Documents. *New Books*. Washington, DC: GPO, 1982 to present. Bimonthly.

United States. Superintendent of Documents. *U.S. Government Books*. Washington, DC: GPO, 1982 to present. Quarterly.

#### *Periodicals*

Andriot, John, editor. *Guide to United States Government Serials and Periodicals*. McLean, Virginia: Documents Index, 1969 to present. Annual.

*Index to U.S. Government Periodicals*. Chicago: Infordata International, 1970 to present. Quarterly.

United States. Superintendent of Documents. *Price List 36*. Washington, DC: GPO, 1973 to present.

## Subject Bibliographies

United States. Superintendent of Documents. *Subject Bibliographies.* Washington, DC: GPO, 1975 to present.
United States. Superintendent of Documents. *Subject Bibliography Index.* Washington, DC: GPO, 1975 to present.

## General Sources

United States. Superintendent of Documents. *GPO New Sales Publications.* Washington, DC: GPO, 1971 to present. Monthly.
United States. Superintendent of Documents. *GPO Sales Publications Reference File.* Washington, DC: GPO, 1971 to present. Bimonthly.
United States. Superintendent of Documents. *Monthly Catalog of United States Government Publications.* Washington, DC: GPO, 1895 to present. Monthly.

## Statistics

Congressional Information Service. *American Statistics Index.* Washington, DC: Congressional Information Service, 1974 to present. Monthly.

## Technical Reports

United States. Department of Commerce. National Technical Information Service. *Government Reports Announcements and Index.* Springfield, Virginia: National Technical Information Service, 1946 to present. Semimonthly.
United States. Department of Commerce. National Technical Information Service. *Government Reports Annual Index.* Springfield, Virginia: National Technical Information Service, 1946 to present. Annual.

## Reference Sources and Directories

*Encyclopedia of Governmental Advisory Organizations.* 5th edition, Detroit, Michigan: Gale Research, 1985.
*Federal Executive Directory.* Washington, DC: Carroll Publishing, 1986. Annual.
*Federal Regulatory Directory.* Washington, DC: Congressional Quarterly, 1979/1980 to present. Annual.
*Federal Staff Directory.* Mount Vernon, Virginia: Congressional Staff Directory, 1986. Annual.
*Federal Yellow Book.* Washington, DC: Washington Monitor, 1986.
National Archives. Office of the Federal Register. *United States Government Manual.* Washington, DC: GPO, 1935 to present. Annual.
*Washington Information Directory.* Washington, DC: Congressional Quarterly, 1975/1976 to present. Annual.
Whitnah, Donald R., editor. *Government Agencies.* Westport, Connecticut: Greenwood, 1983.

## Congressional Information

Commerce Clearing House. *Congressional Index.* Chicago: Commerce Clearing House, 1937/1938 to present. Twice weekly.
Congressional Information Service. *CIS Index to Publications of the United States Congress.* Washington, DC: Congressional Information Service, 1970 to present. Monthly.
Congressional Information Service. *CIS Legislative History Service.* Washington, DC: Congressional Information Service, 1974 to present. Annual.
*Congressional Quarterly Almanac.* Washington, DC: Congressional Quarterly, 1986. Annual.

*Congressional Quarterly Weekly Report.* Washington, DC: Congressional Quarterly, 1943 to present. Weekly.

*Congressional Roll Call.* Washington, DC: Congressional Quarterly, 1986. Annual.

*Congressional Staff Directory.* Mount Vernon, Virginia: Congressional Staff Directory, 1959 to present. Annual.

*Congressional Yellow Book.* Washington, DC: Washington Monitor, 1986.

Dialog Information Services. Congressional Records Abstracts. Washington, DC: Capitol Services, 1981 to present. Database.

United States. *United States Code. Congressional and Administrative News.* Washington, DC: GPO, 1951 to present.

United States. Congress. *Congressional Record.* Washington, DC: GPO, 1873 to present.

United States. Congress. *Official Congressional Directory.* Washington, DC: GPO, 1986. Annual.

United States. Library of Congress. Congressional Research Service. *Digest of Public General Bills and Resolutions.* Washington, DC: GPO, 1936 to present.

## Federal Laws

United States. *United States Code.* Washington, DC: GPO, 1925 to present.

United States. *United States Statutes at Large.* Washington, DC: GPO, 1789 to present.

## Presidential Publications

United States. *Code of Federal Regulations.* Washington, DC: GPO, 1948 to present.

United States. *Federal Register.* Washington, DC: GPO, 1936 to present. Daily except Saturday and Sunday.

United States. *Federal Register Index.* Washington, DC: GPO, 1984 to present.

## United States Budget

United States. *Budget of the U.S. Government.* Washington, DC: GPO, 1986. Annual.

United States. *Catalog of Federal Domestic Assistance.* Washington, DC: GPO, 1986. Annual.

United States. *Major Themes and Additional Detail.* Washington, DC: GPO, 1986. Annual.

United States. *United States Budget in Brief.* Washington, DC: GPO, 1986. Annual.

## State and Local Publications Monthly Checklist

United States. Library of Congress. Processing Services. *Monthly Checklist of State Publications.* Washington, DC: GPO, 1910 to present. Monthly.

## Urban Documents

*Index to Current Urban Documents.* Westport, Connecticut: Greenwood Press, 1972 to present. Quarterly.

## Foreign Documents

Great Britain. Stationery Office. *Government Publications.* London: Her Majesty's Stationery Office, 1923 to present. Monthly.

United Nations. *UNDOC: Current Index.* New York: United Nations, 1979 to present. Monthly except July and August.

## REFERENCE

Morehead, Joe. *Introduction to United States Public Documents.* 3rd edition. Littleton, Colorado: Libraries Unlimited, 1983.

# CHAPTER 8
# Statistics*

A major problem facing social work educators and students as well as practitioners and policy formulators is finding valid statistical data on social welfare and social work. As social work becomes more empirically based, it will no doubt place a greater emphasis on the use of statistical data.

This chapter identifies and describes research resources which contain statistical data useful for social welfare and social work practitioners, educators and students. A brief discussion of the utilization of statistical data in social welfare and social work is followed by a presentation of research tools, such as indexes and abstracts, which may be used to access statistical data and a selective listing and description of primary sources of statistics.

"Social welfare" is used to denote public assistance programs; "social work" for the promotion of the welfare of individuals, groups and communities by an organized helping profession; and "statistics" for quantitative social indicators.

## SOCIAL INDICATORS

Two types of statistical data are used by social workers. One type illustrates aspects of a specific topic at a particular time while the other type depicts major trends of important social phenomena over time.

Social indicators are useful for different persons: program administrators monitoring specific programs; beneficiaries of programs; their representatives and lobbyists, who need accurate data for monitoring programs and proposing changes; policymakers in government, who need data for legislating and implementing change; and students and scholars studying the welfare state (Hauser, 1975, p. 137).

Quantative data on federally funded public assistance and Social Security programs are collected and utilized in the attempt to find out how the programs are operating (descriptive statistics), how well they meet their objective (evaluative statistics), and how they could be improved (statistics for the analysis of alternative policies) (Hauser, 1975, p. 137). Thus, quantitative data provide a statistical picture of the factors influencing welfare planning and policy formulation.

No comprehensive delineation of criteria for the use of social welfare and social work statistics is to be found in the social work journal literature, but a useful set of criteria for the use of criminal justice statistics was set forth in the *Challenge of Crime in a Free Society,* the summary report of the President's Commission on Law

*Parts of this chapter were originally published as "Sources of Social Work and Social Welfare Statistics," *Reference Services Review* 14 (1) (Spring 1986): 41–47, and are reprinted with the permission of Pierian Press.

Enforcement and the Administration of Justice in 1965. Many of the same criteria may be applied to social work and social welfare. Thus, with some modification of the Commission's criteria, social indicators for social welfare and social work should do the following: (1) inform the public and those persons responsible for policy formulation about the nature of social problems, their magnitude and their trends over time; (2) measure the effects of social programs and policies from the local to the national level; (3) indicate who needs help and divide such information into sociodemographic variables, such as age, sex, race, socioeconomic status, neighborhood, etc., in order to help focus social welfare programs; (4) measure the work load and effectiveness of social agencies and state and federal programs; (5) analyze the factors contributing to success and failure of social programs; (6) provide social welfare agencies with comparative norms of performance; (7) assess direct public expenditures by social welfare programs and agencies; (8) furnish baseline data for research; (9) project social problems and social welfare trends and their consequences into the future for better planning; (10) assess the societal and other causes of social welfare problems to develop theoretical perspectives for social welfare and social work; (11) analyze the effectiveness of social casework methods; and (12) measure the quality of life both at the local and national levels.

Some of the data needed to meet the criteria are available from a number of sources. However, much of them are not available. Schreiber and Fanshel (1977) enumerate several reasons for the unavailability of such data. They mention the "methodological difficulties inherent in measuring qualitative changes in complex social arenas and to the lack of agreement on what constitutes a set of reliable and valid criteria." They also mention the problem of indifference among many practitioners and administrators to the use and value of statistics. Another problem is the lack of any central agency or organization that could collect, regulate and standardize statistics. Attempts to set up statistical reporting systems for social agencies have not been successful.

The federal government has been more successful in data collection than have nonfederal social welfare organizations and agencies. Social Security laws (Social Security Act, 1935) require reporting of data, and this has resulted in numerous data series that enable one to trace the growth and development of public assistance, the social insurances, and the child health and welfare services.

One result of compulsory reporting of data by the states is uniform, standardized series of data on categorical assistance and unemployment insurance. Data on old age, survivors and disability insurance have emanated directly from federal agencies. Thus, statistical data for public welfare expenditures are much more readily available than are data from the private sector. For example, the Social Security system provides the bulk of its own statistics, which are reported in the *Social Security Bulletin.*

Schreiber and Fanshel have included numerous tables illustrating "a rudimentary statistical framework within which social welfare operates." A cursory glance at the tables shows that social welfare and social work are concerned with a wide variety of social phenomena and consequently a wide variety of data to describe or indicate those phenomena. The rest of this chapter serves as a guide to sources of statistical data.

## BIBLIOGRAPHIC CONTROL LITERATURE

The following indexing and abstracting services, although previously described in Chapter 3, "Journal and Newspaper Articles," as tools for finding journal articles, also serve as tools for finding statistical data. Discussion of these sources focuses on their usefulness for locating such data.

*Social Work Research and Abstracts (SWRA)*: A search of its index for a 19-year period showed that the term "statistics" was used twice, "social indicators" 13 times. Evidently, social workers write very little specifically about the use of statistics and social indicators in social work and social welfare. Many research articles contain data on specific topics, but it is difficult if not impossible to know which articles contain which data without looking up each article. Abstracts of articles usually mention hypothesis, sample size and major findings but do not describe data tables. This shortcoming is not unique to *SWRA* but is true for most abstracting services in the social sciences.

*Journal of Human Services Abstracts (JHSA)*: This abstracting service covers statistical data slightly better than does *SWRA*. Three index terms for statistics have been used since its inception in 1976. In order to find articles about statistics or social indicators one would look under "social indicators," "social indicators research" or "statistical data needed for planning." While *JHSA* indexes a wider variety of materials than *SWRA*, which focuses primarily on journal articles, it is probably *JHSA*'s emphasis on the management of human services that has led to better coverage of studies concerned with social indicators and the utilization of statistics.

*Social Welfare, Social Planning/Policy and Social Development: An International Database (SOPODA)*: Section Two, "Social Planning/Policy," contains a section, listed in the table of contents, entitled "Social Indicators." The same term also appears as an index term, as do "statistics," "statistical," and "statistically." The section on social indicators contains abstracts of articles from such journals as the *Journal of Social Policy, Social Indicators Research,* and *Social Policy and Administration.*

*Psychological Abstracts (PA)*: Although *PA* has no index term for social indicators, there are numerous terms for statistics: "statistical analysis," "statistical correlation," "statistical data," "statistical measurement," "statistical norms," "statistical sample parameters," "statistical samples," "statistical significance," "statistical tables," "statistical tests," "statistical validity," "statistical variables," and "statistics." There are numerous related terms which may be found by consulting the *Thesaurus of Psychological Index Terms,* 4th edition, a compilation of index terms used in *Psychological Abstracts.*

*Sociological Abstracts (SA)*: Much of the material indexed in *SA* is relevant for social welfare. Pertinent sections are "The Family and Socialization," "Sociology of Health and Medicine," "Social Problems and Social Welfare," "Community Development," "Studies in Poverty," and "Policy, Planning, Forecasting," which contains a subsection on social indicators. The terms "social indicators," "statistics," "statistical" and "statistically" appear in the subject index to allow researchers to narrow literature searches to relevant articles. There is some overlap between *SA* and *SOPODA* but *SOPODA* focuses more on policy-oriented literature than does the more broadly based *SA*.

Several other indexes and abstracting services contain information relevant for social work and social welfare but do not cover the social work literature as thoroughly as do the ones described above. Articles containing statistical data might be found in such indexes and abstracts as *Social Sciences Citation Index, Sage Family Studies Abstracts, Human Resources Abstracts, Social Sciences Index, Public Affairs Information Service, Urban Affairs Abstracts* and *Women Studies Abstracts.*

Except for *JHSA* and *SOPODA*, the traditional bibliographic control mechanisms for the social and behavioral sciences offer little help to social work researchers seeking statistical data on social indicators concerned exclusively with social work issues. Social work journals are not adequately covered in most social science indexes and abstracting services, and locating statistical data is not as straightforward as it should be. Abstracts of articles (in abstracting services) seldom indicate what data are contained in an article.

## DATABASES

Chapter 5 discussed the advantages of computerized literature searches and the similarities of databases to print indexes. Databases are not much more useful for retrieving statistical data than are print indexes. They do offer the flexibility of combining index terms, but because little attempt is made to denote statistical studies in either print or online indexes, their usefulness is limited.

A few databases do contain statistical manipulation features, but they are primarily business oriented and of little use to social workers. One database that might be useful is CENDATA, produced by the U.S. Bureau of Census. It contains "selected statistical data, press releases, and product information from the Bureau of Census." Presently specializing in "time-sensitive information," CENDATA is supposed to evolve into "a comprehensive compendium" of Census Bureau data. When it does, it may prove to be a quick access tool to census data.

## REFERENCE SOURCES AND PRIMARY SOURCES

A researcher may be familiar with a few primary sources of statistical information, such as a particular organization or government publication. But if a needed data source is not known or if it is necessary to consult all potential data sources, it may be necessary to initially consult a reference source that will guide the researcher to primary sources. The process contains two steps: (1) determining if statistics are available on a particular topic and (2) locating and gaining access to the primary source.

Statistical data and social indicators have traditionally been difficult to track down. The above-described bibliographic control mechanisms do not suffice for gleaning data from the literature. Due to the inadequacy of existing sources, several newer reference sources have been developed that will lead the researcher to primary sources of data. A few reference sources actually contain primary data. Nonfederal sources are described below, and federal data sources are described in the next section.

### Nonfederal

*American Statistics Index (ASI)* is a monthly with annual cumulations. It attempts to be a master guide and index to all the statistical publications of the U.S. government, particularly publications that contain primary data of research value or secondary data collected on a special subject and also special studies and analyses or other statistics-related materials. *ASI* is issued in two sections: The index has references to abstract accession numbers which must then be looked up in the abstracts section, which contains full descriptions of the content and format of each publication. *ASI* contains abstracts of many statistical publications not available through the GPO or its *Monthly Catalog* (described below). The index is comprised of four subindexes: subject and name, category, title, and agency report number.

Because the U.S. government is the world's most important and prolific publisher of statistics, the inception of *ASI* in 1972 marked an important milestone in the control of and access to the myriad federal publications. It was created to meet the need expressed by the 1971 President's Commission on Federal Statistics for "a central catalog of data available in government agencies." *ASI* accomplishes this goal by identifying the statistical data published by all branches and agencies of the federal government. It catalogs the publications in which these data appear, providing full bibliographic information about each publication; announces new publications as they appear; describes the contents of the publications; indexes information in detail by subject; and micropublishes most of the indexed publications.

*ASI's* coverage of social welfare, social work and Social Security statistical publications is extensive. It covers all agencies that produce statistical publications of the Department of Health and Human Services, including Health Resources and Services Administration; National Center for Health Statistics; National Center for Health Services Research; Health Services Administration; National Institute of Health; Alcohol, Drug Abuse and Mental Health Administration; Office of Human Development Services; Health Care Financing Administration; and Social Security Administration. Also included are statistical publications of the Department of Education; Department of Housing and Urban Development; Department of Justice; Department of Labor; Department of Commerce, which includes the Bureau of Census and other departments; as well as independent agencies, special boards, committees and commissions, U.S. courts and the U.S. Congress.

The easiest way to locate pertinent documents is to start with the subject and name index. One may look under the names of specific agencies, e.g., Office of Human Development Services or Health Care Financing Administration, or under subject terms, such as quality of life, Social Security, Social Security Act, Social Security Administration, Social Security Tax, and Social Services. Entries under these terms are numerous, and a scanning of the titles listed under the broad subject terms will provide a researcher with a good overview of what statistical information the federal government publishes.

Detailed abstracts may then be found in the volume containing abstracts by looking up the *ASI* accession number. Accession numbers correspond to issuing agency, thus grouping together all publications issued by a particular agency. For instance, one would look under "Department of Health and Human Services" to find all of their statistical publications. Their general publications are listed first and the rest by issuing agency. The 1982 abstracts volume contains 85 pages of abstracts of the statistical publications of the Department of Health and Human Services.

*Statistical Reference Index: A Selective Guide to American Statistical Publications from Private Organizations and State Government Sources (SRI)* is a monthly with annual cumulations. It serves as a master index to the myriad and voluminous statistical publications of U.S. private organizations, state governments and their agencies, associations, commercial publishers, business organizations, independent research centers, and universities. Included are national and statewide data, data on foreign countries, local and narrowly focused data.

*SRI* is published in two sections, the index and the abstracts. The latter is accessed by accession numbers found in the index. The index is arranged by subjects and names, categories, issuing sources, and titles. Because *SRI* is published by the same organization that publishes *ASI*, it is organized and used in much the same fashion. Subject entry terms are the same as in *ASI*. The types of statistical publications collected and indexed by *SRI* were difficult to obtain until CIS began this index. The beginning of the abstracts section lists the many and diverse issuing sources which CIS monitors in order to collect its statistical publications.

*Index to International Statistics: A Guide to the Statistical Publications of International Intergovernmental Organizations (IIS)* indexes and abstracts current English-language statistical publications of the world's international intergovernmental organizations. Included are organizations of the United Nations, the Organization for Economic Cooperation and Development, the Organization of American States, the European Community, development banks and special purpose organizations. Coverage focuses on "basic economic, demographic, industrial and social statistics of general research value and national, international, or worldwide scope."

The types of statistical publications *IIS* indexes include primary data on business, finance, economic development, agriculture, foreign trade, transportation, communication, energy, health, employment, education, government, and natural resources. Access is provided through five indexes: subjects, names and geographic areas; categories; issuing agencies; titles; and publication numbers.

Social welfare researchers should find *IIS* a useful means of finding international and comparative social welfare data. Subject index terms include "social development," "community development," "health resources development," and "urban development."

*The Municipal Year Book* is an annual publication which presents a wide array of data on municipal government. The data come from surveys conducted by the International City Management Association as well as additional sources. Data tables are accompanied by text which presents "thoughtful analysis and timely information." Five sections cover local government profiles: the international dimension, personnel issues, management issues and trends, directories, and references. Data are presented on health care, housing, human services, affirmative action, education, personnel, welfare programs, law enforcement, minority groups, and Social Security.

*The Book of the States* is a biennial publication of the Council of State Governments. The Council conducts research on state programs and problems as one of its activities. This publication presents information and data on the structures, working methods, financing and functional activities of state governments. In it social welfare researchers will find useful data on human services, such as aid to families with dependent children, general assistance, public health, education, housing and development.

## Federal

*Statistical Abstract of the United States: National Database and Guide to Sources* is the standard summary of quantitative data about the United States. It is also one of the oldest such publications. Included are data on population, vital statistics, health and nutrition, education, law enforcement, state and local government, social insurance, and human services and comparative international statistics. This one-volume sourcebook is an excellent ready-reference tool since it contains so much data on so many subjects. A particularly useful feature is the footnotes to most of the tables which refer the reader to the primary source from which the table was taken. Included in the appendices is a "Guide to Sources of Statistics." Statistical series of the U.S. government are listed and arranged by subject. For example, listed under "social insurance" and "human services" are numerous statistical reporting series. A section following the "Guide to Sources of Statistics" lists guides to state statistical abstracts.

*The State and Metropolitan Area Data Book* (1986) is a handy, one-volume compilation of data on state and metropolitan areas in the United States. Statistics included represent generally useful summary measures that are available in comparable form for the geographic areas covered. Each chapter or section has a similar arrangement of tables. Table A covers metropolitan areas and components, which are listed in alphabetical order. Tables cover the whole range of available statistics, including social insurance and welfare. Table B covers central cities of SMSAs. Table C covers regions, divisions and states.

*The County and City Data Book* (1983) is billed as a supplement to the *Statistical Abstract of the United States.* It presents "statistical data for each county in the U.S., 277 SMSA's as of June, 1977 and each of the 910 cities of 25,000 inhabitants or more in 1975." Data are also given for standard federal administrative regions, census regions and divisions and states.

*The Handbook of Labor Statistics* is an annual which includes data presented in tabular form on wages and salaries, prices, unemployment, Social Security, health care costs, etc., as they relate to labor.

*Social Indicators III: Selected Data on Social Conditions and Trends in the United States* is the latest volume in an irregular series. It gives comprehensive statistical data on Social Security and welfare benefits, housing, social participation, health and nutrition, family size and composition, work and numerous other topics of interest to social workers. Data are presented in tabular and graphic form. The two earlier titles in this series are *Social Indicators, 1976: Selected Data on Social Conditions and Trends in the United States* and *Social Indicators, 1973: Selected Data on Social Conditions and Trends in the United States*.

*Historical Statistics of the United States, Colonial Times to 1970* is the third in a series of guides to historical statistics published by the Bureau of the Census as a supplement to the annual *Statistical Abstract of the United States*. The first volume in the series covered the years 1789 to 1945 and was published in 1949. The second volume covered colonial times to 1957, was published in 1960, and substantially expanded on the data included in the first volume. The most recent volume supersedes the earlier works. Its objective is to collect and refer. The first function "consists of assembling, selecting and arranging data from hundreds of sources and making them available within a single source. The referring function consists of text annotations to the data which act as a guide to sources of greater detail." Sections of interest to social welfare researchers include "Population," "Vital Statistics and Health and Medical Care," "Migration," "Consumer Income and Expenditures," and "Social Statistics." The chapter "Social Statistics: Social Security and Welfare" starts with a lengthy introduction to and explanation of the federal government's historical efforts to collect social welfare statistics and of the sources consulted in order to compile the volume. Numerous tables are presented with annotations providing definitions of terms and notes on resources.

*The Sourcebook of Criminal Justice Statistics* has been an annual publication since 1973. It is a compilation of criminal justice and related statistics available in a variety of publications from governmental and private agencies. It is nationwide in scope and has six sections: "Criminal Justice System Characteristics," "Public Attitudes Towards Crime," "Nature of Known Offenses," "Persons Arrested," "Judicial Processing," and "Correctional Supervision." An appendix lists sources and has annotations describing the sources.

## Selected U.S. Government Statistical Series

In addition to the above-described sources, the U.S. government publishes regular and irregular statistical series on numerous topics of interest to social work and social welfare. Following is a selective listing of federal statistical publications arranged by issuing agency. Publications included are ones that are relevant for social work and social welfare. The numbers following the titles are SuDocs series numbers that are used to locate the publications in a collection of federal publications.

### *Department of Commerce*

The Department of Commerce, U.S. Bureau of the Census, publishes *Current Population Reports* (C 3.186). The Bureau of the Census uses this series and those noted below to update the decennial census. Reports in these series are issued either on a periodic or irregular basis.

*Current Population Reports* are monthly nationwide surveys providing data on population counts, characteristics, etc. Separate series and their numbers include *Population Characteristics* (P-20), *Special-Studies* (P-23), *Federal State Cooperative Program for Population Estimates* (P-26), *Population Estimates and Projections* (P-25), *Farm Population* (P-27), *Special Census* (P-28), and *Consumer Income* (P-60). A tremendous amount of data is included in the *Current Population Reports Series*. Data may be found on such topics as geographical mobility, school enrollment, fertility of American women, marital status and living arrangements, child support and alimony, and work disability.

*Current Housing Reports* (C 3.215) series provides statistics on housing characteristics. Related series include *Housing Vacancies* (H-111), *Housing Characteristics* (H-121), and *Market Absorption of Apartments* (H-130). Every two years there is an *Annual Housing Survey* (AHS) (H-170-83), which is a national sample of housing units and a metropolitan area survey of housing units. It is conducted by the Census Bureau for the Department of Housing and Urban Development. Results of the *AHS* are contained in six annual reports: *General Housing Characteristics, Indicators of Housing and Neighborhood Quality, Financial Characteristics of the Housing Inventory, Housing Characteristics of Recent Movers, Urban and Rural Housing Characteristics,* and *Energy-Related Housing Characteristics.*

There are three other publications of the Census Bureau that social welfare researchers should find useful. A monthly publication entitled *Data User News* (C 3.238) is aimed at small-area data users. Issues contain brief articles on CB products, services and activities, new uses of CB data, small-area data activities of other government agencies, and Summary Tape Processing Centers throughout the country. The *Directory of Computerized Data Files* (C 3.262) is a loose-leaf directory of Census Bureau holdings of computer data files from censuses, surveys, and administrative records. The *Monthly Product Announcement* (C 3.163) is a monthly listing of CB publications, microfiche, and data files issued during the previous month.

### Department of Health and Human Services (HHS)

*Child Support Enforcement: Annual Report to Congress* (HE 24.1) is a publication of HHS issued annually. It contains data on caseloads and collection activities of the Child Support Enforcement Program under Title IV-D of the Social Security Act.

*Financial Assistance by Geographic Area* (HE 1.57) is an annual report presenting data for each state, local government or private institution receiving financial assistance under all HHS domestic assistance programs. This report is issued in 10 volumes.

The *Publication Catalog of HHS* (HE 1.18) is an annual annotated list of HHS publications in the fields of health services, mental health, education, social and rehabilitation services, and Social Security.

### HHS. Health Resources and Services Administration

*Public Health Reports* (HE 20.6011) is a bimonthly journal of public health which contains feature articles, short items and research reports on numerous health topics.

### HHS. National Center for Health Statistics

*Monthly Vital Statistics Report Provisional Data* (HE 20.6217) has monthly provisional tabulations of births, marriages, divorces, and deaths. Final tabulation is published annually with a three- to four-year time lag. For example, data for 1978 are published in 1982. *Vital Statistics of the United States* is the annual tabulation of

*Monthly Vital Statistics*. It is a multivolume publication broken down into parts. For instance, the 1978 annual published in 1982 covers mortality in Volume II, Part A. *Monthly Vital Statistics Report, Annual Summary of Births, Deaths, Marriages and Divorces* (HE 20.6217) is an annual summary of the monthly provisional data.

*Vital and Health Statistics Series* presents data from the National Vital Statistics System and the National Health Survey. It consists of hundreds of reports divided among 13 active series: *Programs and Collection Procedures* (HE 20:6209:1); *Data Evaluation and Methods Research* (HE 20.620:2); *Analytical and Epidemiological Studies* (HE 20.6209:B); *Documents and Committee Reports* (HE 20.609:4); *Data from the National Health Interview Survey* (HE 20.6209:10); *Data from the National Health Examination Survey and National Health and Nutrition Examination Survey* (HE 20.6209:11); *Data on Health Resources Utilization* (H# 20.6209:13); *Data on Health Resources: Manpower and Facilities* (HE 20.6209:14); *Data from Special Surveys* (HE 20.6209:15); *Data on Mortality* (HE 20.6209:20); *Data on Nationality Marriage and Divorce* (HE 20.6209.21); and *Data from the National Survey of Family Growth* (HE 20.6209.23).

## HHS. National Institute on Alcohol Abuse and Alcoholism

*Alcohol Health and Research World* (HE 20.8309) is a quarterly journal on the study and treatment of alcoholism. Articles often include statistical data on patients' demographic and personality characteristics. *National Drug and Alcoholism Treatment Utilization Survey* (HE 20.8302), published biennially, reports on the characteristics, utilization, staff, and funding of alcoholism treatment services.

## HHS. National Institute on Drug Abuse

The *National Survey on Drug Abuse* is based on a biennial household survey of the prevalence and frequency of illegal drug use, medical and nonmedical use of prescription drugs, alcohol use and cigarette smoking. The most recently issued report is entitled "Main Findings, 1982" (HE 20.8202.Su 7/982).

## HHS. National Institute of Mental Health

*Information Systems Reports,* Series FN (HE 20.8110) is a continuing series of studies and reports on mental health facility information systems, focusing primarily on uses for multiservice facilities in the Community Mental Health Centers Program. These reports review and evaluate planning, acquisition, implementation, uses, and cost effectiveness of various systems in terms of community mental health center finances, management and clinical requirements, and patient needs.

*Mental Health National Statistics,* Series CN (HE 20.8110) is another series of reports focusing on mental health facilities, services, staff, and patient characteristics.

## HHS. Health Care Financing Administration

*Health Care Financing Review* (HE 22.18) is a quarterly journal devoted to presenting data on health care expenditures, specifically the Medicaid and Medicare programs, and research on health care financing.

*Medicare: Use of Health Services* (HE 22.19), *Medicare Program Statistics Annual* (HE 22.19), *Medicare: Use of Short-Stay Hospitals by Aged and Disabled Inpatients* (HE 22.19), and *Medicare: Participating Providers and Suppliers of Health Services* (HE 22.19) present detailed data on Medicare enrollment, utilization, reimbursement and participating facilities.

## HHS. Social Security Administration (SSA)

*Social Security Administration Annual Report to the Congress* covers activities and program operations, with comparative data for previous years. *Characteristics of State Plans for Aid to Families with Dependent Children* (HE 3.2: C43) is the annual report on provisions of AFDC programs.

## HHS. SSA. Office of Research, Statistics and International Policy

*Social Security Bulletin* (HE 3.3) is a monthly journal which presents information and statistics on current Social Security program development and historical data from 1940 or the year a program began. Contents include Social Security in review, summarizing recent legislation and program operations; feature articles, notes and brief reports; current operating statistics; and quarterly statistics.

*Social Security Bulletin Annual Statistical Supplement* (HE 3.313: 1982), an annual report, cumulates the data reported in the *Monthly Bulletin.*

*Public Assistance Recipients in Standard Metropolitan Statistical Areas* (HE 3.6112: 982) is an annual report covering recipients under AFDC and state/local general assistance programs by SMSA, county, and state.

*Proceedings: National Workshop on Welfare Research and Statistics* (HE 3/2: W45/4) is published irregularly. The 22nd National Workshop had as a theme "Welfare Research and Statistics, a Foundation for the Future." Numerous welfare topics are covered.

### Department of Housing and Urban Development (HUD)

*Urban Development Action Grants, Quarterly Awards* is a quarterly press release series which announces preliminary approvals of Urban Development Action Grants to local areas. There are two press releases in this series: *Awards to Metropolitan Cities* and *Awards to Small Cities.* Each release includes brief project descriptions as well as statistical data.

*Financing for Elderly Handicapped Housing by HUD: News Release* is an annual press release describing allocation of loan money to projects providing rental housing and related facilities to elderly and disabled persons.

## HUD. Community Planning and Development

*Community Development Block Grant Program, Directory of Allocations for FY 80–85* is an irregularly issued annual report providing data on allocation of funds for Community Development Block Grants.

## CONCLUSION

It can be seen from the numerous sources described above that social work and social welfare data are available from a variety of sources and in a variety of formats. The most difficult type of data to retrieve is that contained in journal articles, because abstracts of articles seldom mention or go into detailed descriptions of data. Data generated by the federal government are more readily located and available and generally more comprehensive and inclusive than are nonfederal sources.

## SOURCES DISCUSSED

### Bibliographic Control Literature

American Psychological Association. *Psychological Abstracts.* Washington, DC: American Psychological Association. Monthly with semiannual cumulations, 1927 to present.

National Association of Social Workers. *Social Work Research and Abstracts.* Albany, New York: National Association of Social Workers. Quarterly with annual cumulations.

Project Share. *Journal of Human Services Abstracts.* Rockville, Maryland: Project Share. Irregular, 1976 to present.

Sociological Abstracts. *Social Welfare, Social Planning/Policy and Social Development: An International Database.* San Diego, California: Sociological Abstracts. Triannual.

Sociological Abstracts. *Sociological Abstracts.* San Diego, California: Sociological Abstracts. Monthly with annual cumulations.

### Databases

U.S. Department of Commerce. Bureau of the Census. CENDATA. Online database. Availability: Dialog.

### Reference Sources and Primary Sources

#### Nonfederal

*American Statistics Index.* Washington, DC: Congressional Information Service. Monthly with annual cumulations.

Council of State Governments. *Book of the States.* Lexington, Kentucky: The Council of State Governments. Annual.

*Index to International Statistics.* Washington, DC: Congressional Information Service. Monthly with annual cumulations.

International Management Association. *Municipal Yearbook.* Washington, DC: International City Management Association. Annual.

*Statistical Reference Index.* Washington, DC: Congressional Information Service. Monthly with annual cumulations.

#### Federal

U.S. Department of Commerce. Bureau of the Census. *County and City Data Book.* Washington, DC: GPO, 1983.

U.S. Department of Commerce. Bureau of the Census. *Historical Statistics of the United States, Colonial Times to 1970.* Washington, DC: GPO, 1975.

U.S. Department of Commerce. Bureau of the Census. *Social Indicators III: Selected Data in Social Conditions and Trends in the United States.* Washington, DC: GPO, 1980.

U.S. Department of Commerce. Bureau of the Census. *State and Metropolitan Area Data Book.* Washington, DC: GPO, 1986.

U.S. Department of Commerce. Bureau of the Census. *Statistical Abstract of the United States: National Database and Guide to Sources.* Washington, DC: GPO. Annual.

U.S. Department of Justice. National Criminal Justice Reference Service. *Sourcebook of Criminal Justice Statistics.* Washington, DC: GPO. Annual.

U.S. Department of Labor. Bureau of Labor Statistics. *Handbook of Labor Statistics.* Washington, DC: GPO. Annual.

## Selected U.S. Government Statistical Series

### Department of Commerce

U.S. Department of Commerce. Bureau of the Census. *Annual Housing Survey.* Washington, DC: GPO. Biennial.
U.S. Department of Commerce. Bureau of the Census. *Current Housing Reports.* Washington, DC: GPO. Biennial.
U.S. Department of Commerce. Bureau of the Census. *Current Population Reports.* Washington, DC: GPO. Irregular.
U.S. Department of Commerce. Bureau of the Census. *Data User News.* Washington, DC: GPO. Monthly.
U.S. Department of Commerce. Bureau of the Census. *Directory of Computerized Data Files.* Washington, DC: GPO. Annual.
U.S. Department of Commerce. Bureau of the Census. *Monthly Product Announcements.* Washington, DC: GPO. Monthly.

### Department of Health and Human Services (HHS)

U.S. Department of Health and Human Services. *Child Support Enforcement: Annual Report to Congress.* Washington, DC: GPO. Annual.
U.S. Department of Health and Human Services. *Financial Assistance by Geographic Area.* Washington, DC: GPO. Annual.
U.S. Department of Health and Human Services. *Publication Catalog of HHS.* Washington, DC: GPO. Annual.

### HHS. Health Resources and Services Administration

U.S. Department of Health and Human Services. Health Resources and Services Administration. *Public Health Reports.* Washington, DC: GPO. Bimonthly.

### HHS. National Center for Health Statistics

U.S. Department of Health and Human Services. National Center for Health Statistics. *Monthly Vital Statistics Report Provisional Data; Monthly Vital Statistics Report, Annual Summary of Births, Deaths, Marriages and Divorces.* Washington, DC: GPO. Monthly.
U.S. Department of Health and Human Services. National Center for Health Statistics. *Vital and Health Statistics Series.* Washington, DC: GPO.
U.S. Department of Health and Human Services. National Center for Health Statistics. *Vital Statistics of the United States.* Washington, DC: GPO. Annual.

### HHS. National Institute on Alcohol Abuse and Alcoholism

U.S. Department of Health and Human Services. National Institute on Alcohol Abuse and Alcoholism. *Alcohol, Health and Research World.* Washington, DC: GPO. Quarterly.
U.S. Department of Health and Human Services. National Institute on Alcohol Abuse and Alcoholism. *National Drug and Alcoholism Treatment Utilization Survey.* Washington, DC: GPO. Biennial.

### HHS. National Institute on Drug Abuse

U.S. Department of Health and Human Services. National Institute on Drug Abuse. *National Survey on Drug Abuse, Main Findings, 1982.* Washington, DC: GPO. Biennial.

## HHS. *National Institute of Mental Health*

U.S. Department of Health and Human Services. National Institute of Mental Health. *Information Systems Reports,* Series FN. Washington, DC: GPO. Irregular.

U.S. Department of Health and Human Services. National Institute of Mental Health. *Mental Health National Statistics,* Series CN. Washington, DC: GPO. Irregular.

## HHS. *Health Care Financing Administration*

U.S. Department of Health and Human Services. Health Care Financing Administration. *Health Care Financing Review.* Washington, DC: GPO. Quarterly.

U.S. Department of Health and Human Services. Health Care Financing Administration. *Medicare: Use of Health Services, Medicare Program Statistics Annual, Medicare: Use of Short-Stay Hospitals by Aged and Disabled Inpatients; Medicare: Participating Providers and Suppliers of Health Services.* Washington, DC: GPO. Irregular.

## HHS. *Social Security Administration (SSA)*

U.S. Department of Health and Human Services. Social Security Administration. *Characteristics of State Plans for Aid to Families with Dependent Children.* Washington, DC: GPO. Annual.

U.S. Department of Health and Human Services. Social Security Administration. *Social Security Administration Annual Report to the Congress.* Washington, DC: GPO. Annual.

## HHS. SSA. *Office of Research, Statistics and International Policy*

U.S. Department of Health and Human Services. Office of Research, Statistics and International Policy. Social Security Administration. *Proceedings: National Workshop on Welfare Research and Statistics.* Washington, DC: GPO. Irregular.

U.S. Department of Health and Human Services. Office of Research, Statistics and International Policy. Social Security Administration. *Public Assistance Recipients in Standard Metropolitan Statistical Areas.* Washington, DC: GPO. Annual.

U.S. Department of Health and Human Services. Office of Research, Statistics and International Policy. Social Security Administration. *Social Security Bulletin.* Washington, DC: GPO. Monthly.

U.S. Department of Health and Human Services. Office of Research, Statistics and International Policy. Social Security Administration. *Social Security Bulletin Annual Statistical Supplement.* Washington, DC: GPO. Annual.

## *Department of Housing and Urban Development (HUD)*

U.S. Department of Health and Human Services. Department of Housing and Urban Development. *Financing for Elderly Handicapped Housing by HUD: News Release.* Washington, DC: GPO. Annual.

U.S. Department of Health and Human Services. Department of Housing and Urban Development. *Urban Development Action Grants, Quarterly Awards.* Washington, DC: GPO. Quarterly.

## HUD. *Community Planning and Development*

U.S. Department of Health and Human Services. Department of Housing and Urban Development. Community Planning and Development. *Community Development Block Grant Program, Directory of Allocations for FY 80–85.* Washington, DC: GPO. Annual.

## REFERENCES

Hauser, Philip Morris. *Social Statistics in Use.* New York: Russell Sage Foundation, 1975.

Schreiber, Paul and David Fanshel. "Statistical Data in Social Work and Social Welfare." In *The Encyclopedia of Social Work,* pp. 1611–1618. Washington, DC: National Association of Social Workers, 1977.

U.S. National Council on Crime and Delinquency. President's Commission on Law Enforcement and Administration of Justice. *The Challenge of Crime in a Free Society.* Washington, DC: GPO. 1967.

# CHAPTER 9
# The Law

This chapter presents a brief introduction to the basic mechanics of legal research and finding tools that aid the process. Social workers and social work students and educators need to have at least a minimal familiarity with how laws are made and how to find out about the law. Legal research can be confusing and time consuming, but if approached with patience and an awareness of how the literature is organized, it need not be overwhelming. Before getting into the legal literature it is necessary to explain how the legal system works. Legal research necessitates an understanding of court organization, statutory and common law, and the search for authority. The legal literature is shaped by its method of publication, so the system of legal publishing is explained. An exposition of the primary sources of law is followed by a discussion of secondary sources and method of legal citation. The central focus is on federal law, but state and local law are also treated.

## THE FEDERAL LEGAL SYSTEM

Article III, Section 1 of the Constitution of the United States states that "the judicial power of the United States, shall be vested in a Supreme Court, and in such inferior courts as The Congress may from time-to-time ordain and establish." The Supreme Court of the United States is the one mandatory court. Congress, the law-making branch of the federal government, formulates the other levels of federal courts.

Below the Supreme Court are the United States courts of appeals. Below these are the district courts. The district courts and the courts of appeals, for the 11 circuits and the District of Columbia, have geographic jurisdictions and, in some cases, issue jurisdiction, e.g., tax court. The geographic jurisdictions, with the exception of the District of Columbia, are regions composed of groups of states.

Below the federal system are the states. Because each state is sovereign, each makes its own laws and legal system with the exception of certain powers that are delegated to the federal government under the Constitution. This means, in effect, that, including the federal system, there are 51 legal systems rather than one.

The roots of federal law are, of course, to be found in the Constitution. Congress passes acts, also referred to as statutes or laws. The President executes and enforces federal law. The judiciary, or court system, interprets the law and tries cases and, when necessary, establishes legal precedents.

States follow a similar process: The legislatures enact laws, governors enforce and execute them, and the courts interpret the law and try cases. States also have a multitiered court system, with lower courts, such as trial courts, appeal courts, and supreme courts, although the terminology may vary.

## STARE DECISIS

Statutory law is enacted by Congress or state legislatures. In addition to statutory law there is the common law. The common law is that body of law which originated and developed in England. It comprises those principles and roles of action applicable to the government and security of persons and property which do not have for their authority statutory laws, i.e., laws passed by legislatures.

Early in English history the custom developed of considering the decisions of courts as legal precedents. Where no statute or specific law existed to cover a specific situation, the courts developed a principle of law applicable to a certain state of facts. Subsequent cases that had similar facts would be decided according to the original precedent. This is the doctrine of stare decisis, and it is one of the cornerstones of the United States legal system. Stare decisis implies fairness: Similar situations should be decided similarly, and judgements should be consistent, not arbitrary. Where specific statutes do not apply, the law becomes embodied in written court decisions.

Written court decisions are referred to as case law. Case law is not always simple. Decisions of lower courts can be appealed to higher courts, which may uphold or overturn decisions. A legal principle may also be changed as political and social conditions change or as a result of action by Congress. Law is not static but changes continuously in order to accommodate a dynamic society. This principle of accommodation can serve to mollify the doctrine of stare decisis.

## PRIMARY AND SECONDARY SOURCES OF LAW

Thus, in common law there are two divisions: primary and secondary. Primary law is found in written constitutions and enactments of legislatures and in the body of law found in the written opinions of the courts. Constitutions and statutes are published in statute books. Court opinions are published in books called court reports. Secondary sources are all other written expressions of the law, such as treatises, law journals that review the law, legal encyclopedias, and dictionaries.

Primary sources are legal authorities. Legal authorities are either statutory laws or court decisions currently in effect. Legal research is the search for authority. It is the search for either a statute or court decision that governs a particular set of facts. If there is no constitutional or statutory law, then the search is for precedential court decisions.

Because courts are restricted by jurisdictions, i.e., geographical areas or by specific issues, the search must first start in the particular jurisdiction involved. If there is no statute or precedent for one jurisdiction then the search moves to other jurisdictions to find law or precedent that can be applied to the case in question.

Finding federal or state statutes is not too difficult since federal laws and state laws are contained in one set of books for federal laws and one set for each state. These sets of laws are called codes. The search for case law and legal precedent or authority is more complex because of the huge number of cases tried every year.

## GETTING STARTED

Before beginning the search for legal authority it is important to determine what is being sought. It is first necessary to identify the legally important facts and legal issues to be researched. For persons not trained in the law this first step can be the hardest.

There are four criteria to keep in mind to help frame the issues. First is the item or subject matter, i.e., the place or property involved; second is the course of action or grounds for defense; third is the relief being sought, i.e., the purpose of the lawsuit or claim; and fourth is the persons or parties involved and their factual and legal status and relationship to each other. This last point is important. The persons or parties involved may comprise a class or group. For example, the persons involved may be illegal aliens. What the persons or parties do may be important. The illegal aliens may be migrant workers. The relationships between the parties or persons may be relevant, e.g., the relationship between migrant workers and their employers. These issues may well provide clues as to where to start the legal search; that is, they may help identify the relevant sources of the law and terminology to use to begin the search. For example, if the issue involves the employer's duty or the state's duty to provide education to the children of migrant workers, then the search might begin with educational laws.

## SEARCH FOR AUTHORITY

The next step is to search for authority. First, it is necessary to look for statutes that may pertain to the case. Many aspects of the relationship between migrant workers and their employers may be governed by laws. One may first look for state laws and then for federal laws. State and federal rules and regulations may also be involved and should be searched.

Statutory law is mandatory authority and takes precedent over case law. However, in many cases the wording of the law may not cover the facts of the case or there may not be an extant law. Remember that jurisdiction is important. The laws of New York do not pertain to California, nor do the decisions of one district court apply to the decisions of a court in a different district.

If there is no governing statute, then it is necessary to search for case law that may provide precedential authority for the problems or issues being researched. It may also be necessary to search secondary sources, such as legal encyclopedias or law journal articles that discuss the issues involved or similar cases. The secondary sources do not carry the weight of authority, but they may help decipher the primary sources, or if no primary source exists they may help build a persuasive argument as to how the situation could be resolved.

## LEGAL PUBLISHING

Before going any further, an explanation of the system of legal publishing is necessary. The manner in which statutes and case law are published determines how legal research is pursued.

The federal government and many states publish official versions of their codes, rules and regulations, and case law. There are also unofficial versions that add editorial features and research aids to statutory and case law. Two private companies dominate legal publishing: the West Publishing Company (hereafter referred to as West) of St. Paul, Minnesota and the Lawyers' Co-operative Publishing Company (hereafter referred to as Lawyers' edition) of Rochester, New York. There are also companies that publish loose-leaf services which emphasize areas of the law requiring frequent updating. The Commerce Clearing House Company (CCH), the Bureau of National Affairs (BNA), and the Prentice-Hall Company (P-H) all publish important loose-leaf services.

A systematic explanation of the official and unofficial publications is presented in the rest of this chapter. Some discussion of sources of federal law and federal legislative histories has been presented in the chapter on government publications, and additional explanation is given here. In addition to the primary sources there is an explanation of secondary sources and legal research aids. Finally, there is an explanation of legal citations. Legal citations employ extensive abbreviations for sources, and frequently used abbreviations appear after the title of each source.

## FEDERAL COURT DECISIONS

As previously noted, the federal court system consists of three main divisions: the Supreme Court (the highest court), the courts of appeals (the intermediate appellate courts), and the district courts (courts of original jurisdictions where trials occur).

All written opinions of the Supreme Court are published in both official and unofficial versions, as are most appellate court decisions. However, not all district court decisions are published. Unpublished cases are often available through the court clerks.

### United States Supreme Court Reports

The official version of Supreme Court cases is the *United States Reports* (*U.S.*), published by the United States Government Printing Office. The opinions of the court concerning the cases brought to it each yearly term are initially published as slip opinions and then published in advance sheets. Finally, at the end of the term the advance sheets are replaced with bound volumes, usually three or four volumes per term.

The Lawyers' edition is *United States Supreme Court Reports* (*U.S. Law. Ed.*). The opinions are the same as in the official version, but the publishers add important editorial features. Each opinion is preceded by a summary and headnotes on relevant points of laws mentioned in the opinion. Each volume contains an appendix which presents, for selected important cases, summaries of the briefs submitted to the court by the attorneys. The editorial staff also annotates the cases. The annotations are articles or essays that discuss significant legal issues in the cases.

West publishes the *Supreme Court Reporter* (*S. Ct*). West also adds its own editorial features and headnotes. West's unique editorial features will be discussed in detail below. Both West and Lawyers' edition issue advance sheets, which are eventually replaced with bound volumes.

West and Lawyers' edition both publish their advance sheets sooner than does the GPO. But because it takes time to add their editorial features there is still some delay, often as long as several weeks. There are two loose-leaf services that publish the opinions within a week of their being issued. One is *United States Law Week* (*U.S. L. Week*), published by the Bureau of National Affairs, and the other is the Commerce Clearing House *Supreme Court Bulletin*. Because of their currentness they are the most useful tools for finding recent decisions of the Supreme Court.

### Lower Federal Court Reports

The Supreme Court hears only a few selected cases that have been appealed to it. If it refuses to hear a case, the case remains as it was decided in the lower court. Most of the work of the federal courts occurs in the district courts (trial courts) and the courts of appeals.

West is the primary publisher of cases which originate in district courts and are referred to appellate courts. Cases prior to 1880 are contained in a series entitled *Federal Cases* (*Fed. Cas.*). Cases after 1880 are in two series. Appellate court cases are reported in the *Federal Reporter* (*Fed. or F.*). Because of the large number of cases not all cases are published. The *Federal Reporter* publishes selected appellate court opinions. Even fewer district court cases are reported. The ones that are published are contained in the *Federal Supplement* (*F. Sup.*).

Because so few lower federal court cases are reported, there are numerous loose-leaf services that report cases concerning specific subjects. Loose-leaf simply refers to the format of the publication, which allows the service to be kept up-to-date. They are usually well organized and provide useful editorial features, such as subject or topical indexes, abstracts of recent legal developments and tables of cases.

Since the loose-leaf services are devoted to specific topics, they are easier to use than the more voluminous reporters, but it is necessary to read the introductions or prefaces to determine the most efficient methods for using them. Several are relevant for social work and other human services. Civil rights issues are reported in *EEOC Compliance Manual* (BNA), *Equal Opportunity in Housing* (P-H), *Fair Employment Practice Series* (BNA), *Housing and Development Reporter* (BNA), *Mental Disability Law Reporter* (American Bar Association), and *U.S. Law Week* (BNA). Criminal law is reported in the *Criminal Law Reporter* (BNA). Domestic relations cases are reported in *Abortion Law Reporter* (National Abortion Rights Action League), *Family Law Reporter* (BNA), and the *Juvenile Law Newsletter* (National Juvenile Law Center). Education law is reported in *Education for the Handicapped Law Report* (Corporate Reorganization Reporter), the *School Law Bulletin* (Quinlin), and the *Education Law Reporter* (West). Two other topical services are the *Poverty Law Reporter* (CCH), and *Women's Rights Law Reporter* (Rutger's Law School).

## STATE COURT DECISIONS AND THE NATIONAL REPORTER SYSTEM

Many states do not publish official versions of their court cases, relying on private publishers. The major reporting service for state cases is the National Reporter System by West. In addition to state cases the National Reporter System also includes federal cases in the West publications *Supreme Court Reporter, Federal Reporter,* and *Federal Supplement.*

State court cases are reported in seven regional reporters. Because New York and California are the most populous and litigious states they have their own reporters, although their cases are also included in the regional reporters. The regional and state reporters are the *Atlantic Reporter (A.), North Eastern Reporter (N.E.), North Western Reporter (N.W.), Pacific Reporter (P.), South Eastern Reporter (S.E.), South Western Reporter (S.W.), Southern Reporter (S.), New York Supplement (N.Y.S.),* and the *California Reporter (Cal. Rptr.).* The reporters provide the full texts of cases. West also adds its editorial features, including headnotes and its Key Number System (explained below under the American Digest System). They contain indexes called tables of cases, which are useful for locating a case when only the name of the case is known but not the series name, volume and page. West also cross-references cases for researchers who have an official citation but not the West citation. A single case may be reported in more than one source and thus have two or more possible citations, called parallel citations.

To find parallel citations West provides the *National Reporter Blue Book,* a multivolume set which lists all state citations alphabetically by state and gives the parallel citation which can be found in the National Reporter System. Finding parallel citations can be complicated. Do not hesitate to ask a librarian trained in legal research for help.

## DIGESTS

As noted earlier, cases published in official and unofficial reporters are chronological, making it difficult if not impossible to locate cases involving a particular subject. Fortunately, there are sets of law books which rearrange cases by subjects. They are referred to as digests. Digests are similar to abstracting services for journal articles. The digests present summaries of the indexed cases rather than the entire texts. The citation to the appropriate reporter is given so the entire case can be found.

The American Digest System from West is one of the most comprehensive digest series. West uses its own classification system, the Key Number System, to arrange cases by subject or point of law. The system divides legal subjects into seven main classes. Each class is further divided into subclasses and each subclass into topics. There are more than 400 topics, each corresponding to a legal concept. The topics are divided into subdivisions, each assigned a key number. The number is preceded by a small symbol resembling a key.

When West receives the transcript of a case, its editors read the case and determine which points of law are discussed in the case. Each point of law is listed at the beginning of the case and assigned a key number. Every time the same point of law is mentioned it receives the same key number. This is useful for persons looking for cases discussing a particular point of law, e.g., abortion law. It is not necessary to read the entire case but merely to look in the headnotes for the appropriate key number and a summation of the point of law as it was discussed in the case.

West has published several digest series. The *Century Digest* covers cases from 1658 to 1896 in 50 volumes. Subsequent digests were issued for 10-year periods and are called decennial digests. For example, the *Eighth Decennial Digest* covers the years 1966–1976. The most recent digest series is entitled the *General Digest*. It is issued monthly. Yearly cumulations are published in bound volumes. It will become the *Ninth Decennial Digest,* covering the years 1976–1986.

In order to find the topic and key number it is easiest to use the Descriptive Word Index, arranged alphabetically by topic and subject. It might take some guess-work to discover the appropriate topic, but it should be no more difficult than using any other index. Each decennial digest has its own Descriptive Word Index. Once you have located the correct topic you will find a one- or two-sentence description of the legal issues in cases related to the topic. The volume and key number needed to look up the cases in the digest are given following the brief descriptions.

Frequently, researchers know of a case that discusses a point of law. An article on welfare rights might mention a particular case that was instrumental in defining welfare rights. The name of the case can be used to find other cases that also discuss welfare rights. Rather than using the Descriptive Word Index you can use the table of cases in each digest series. Look up the name of the case. The appropriate volume and key number are given. When you look up the volume and key number you will find other related cases, if there are any. Even though it sounds complicated, once you have been through this process once or twice, it will begin to make sense.

In addition to the decennial and general digests there are digests for smaller regional areas. West also publishes key number digests for most states, regional digests and digests for federal court opinions. Federal court opinions are contained in *Federal Practice Digest,* which covers cases from 1961 to the present. Earlier years are covered in the *Modern Federal Practice Digest,* 1939–1960, and the *Federal Digest,* cases prior to 1939. There is also the *U.S. Supreme Court Digest* from West. The Lawyers' edition is *U.S. Supreme Court Reports.* It does not, of course, use West's Key Number System. Because many cases are called by their popular names, West publishes volumes for the various sets that are entitled *Tables of Cases by Popular Names.* They refer you to the correct case name and where it can be found.

## ANNOTATED LAW REPORTS

The American Digest System, described earlier, indexes tens of thousands of cases, many of which are not particularly important or do not add anything new to the understanding of law. A more selective reporting system of appellate court decisions published by the Lawyers' Cooperative Publishing Company is *American Law Reports* (*ALR*). It includes only significant cases determined by its editors to contain points of law of general interest. Included with the reported cases are annotations, lengthy essays on the points of law discussed in the cases. They provide further understanding of the importance of the case and its impact on United States law. *ALR* is somewhat analogous to a legal encyclopedia. The annotations discuss each case thoroughly, present general principles deduced from the case, and point out its applicability. They also may cite and discuss preceding cases related to the case in hand.

Like West's digests, *ALR* is divided into chronological series. For example, *ALR 4th* is the fourth series, covering 1980 to date. Selected federal cases are included in *ALR Fed.*, 1969 to date. Each series, including *ALR Fed.*, has its own *Quick Index*. The Quick Indexes are alphabetical arrangements to the annotations in the ALR volumes and are subdivided by topics and facts. The annotations are listed by their titles.

The various series have different means of keeping current. *ALR 3rd* and *ALR 4th* use supplements contained in the back of each volume. After reading a case and its annotations you need only turn to the pocket supplements to locate cases that may have occurred after the case in hand and are related to it. Because the pocket supplements are loosely placed in the back of the bound volumes, they can be easily taken out and replaced with updated versions. Thus, ALR is quite useful in that it presents only those cases its editors deem significant, provides extensive commentary on the cases, and provides a means of determining if the points of law in a case are still valid or have been superseded by subsequent cases.

## FEDERAL LAWS

Finding federal laws is discussed in Chapter 7, "Public Documents," but some repetition is warranted. Once enacted by Congress and signed by the President, new laws are first published as slip laws, i.e., individual copies of the new law. They are eventually published in chronological order in *United States Statutes at Large*. They are later published in a topical arrangement entitled the United States Code.

Because new laws are not always clearly worded, they must be interpreted by the courts as they try cases. These interpretations are important and have led to privately published annotated versions of the *U.S. Code*. West publishes the *United States Code Annotated* (*USCA*). Each code section contains annotations of court decisions which have cited and interpreted it. In addition, it often includes topic and key numbers to help find additional relevant cases. It also provides cross-references to the *Code of Federal Regulations*. There is a detailed index.

The Lawyers' edition is entitled *United States Code Service* (*USCS*). It also provides cross-references to other Lawyers' editions. Both versions are kept up-to-date through the use of pocket supplements. Both have tables of acts by popular names.

## STATE AND MUNICIPAL LAWS

The organization and publication of state and federal laws are similar. Each state legislature publishes all laws passed during current session. They are generically called session laws. Like the *U.S. Code*, state laws are compiled in codes. They may be published officially by the state and/or unofficially by private publishers. Often they are annotated. Indexes are provided. They are kept up-to-date by pocket supplements. It is always important when using any legal service to check to see if what is being used is current.

Local governments are often called municipalities. They usually operate under a charter similar to a constitution. The laws municipalities enact are referred to as ordinances. Ordinances are codified like state and federal laws. Reported cases concerning ordinances and charters are included in state digests and located through the digest's index. Finding legislative histories for federal law is discussed in the chapter on government publications. Finding histories for state legislation is difficult, if not impossible. Some state libraries and archives can provide materials that had a bearing on legislation, such as letters from lobbying organizations. It is best to consult with a librarian when looking for such materials.

## FEDERAL COURT RULES AND PROCEDURES

Lawsuits are conducted in courts according to procedures and rules. In addition to helping courts conduct their business and establishing uniform procedures, they also provide the litigants with information and instruction concerning judicial proceedings.

There are three categories of federal court rules: rules of civil procedure and criminal procedure, the federal rules of appellate procedure, and individual rules of the various courts. Court decisions often establish or interpret court rules. Civil and criminal rules and procedures can be found in the National Reporter System. West publishes *Federal Rules Decisions (FRD)*. It is integrated into the Key Number System. Callaghan and Company publishes *Federal Rules Service,* which contains the full text of all federal court decisions concerning rules of civil procedures; *Federal Rules Digest,* with abstracts and decisions which appear in *Federal Rules Service; Federal Local Court Rules;* and a *Finding Aids Volume.*

Rules of federal procedure for criminal and civil cases can also be found in the *United States Code Annotated* and the *United States Code Service.*

Rules for presenting evidence can be found in the *U.S. Code* and are called federal rules of evidence. They are also in the unofficial versions. Rules for state courts can generally be found in the state code or in the state reports.

## SHEPARD'S CITATIONS

Earlier this chapter discussed the importance of authority. If there is no particular statute governing a set of facts, then it is necessary to look for case law. A court decision in one case may be reversed by the decision of a higher court or overruled by a subsequent decision by the same court. A case cannot be cited as authoritative unless it has first been determined that it is still good law.

The law books that provide the means to check the authority of a case are entitled *Shepard's Citations. Shepard's Citations* can be used to look up a given case to determine if it has been appealed to a higher court, such as the Supreme Court, and affirmed or reversed. It indicates whether a case was cited in another case. *Shepard's Citations* also shows how the decisions of one case were treated in subsequent cases. It provides judicial histories of a case and its treatment by later decisions. Case histories are indicated in Shepard's by abbreviations that are explained in the front of each volume.

Virtually every set of reporters has a companion Shepard's volume. For example, *Shepard's Federal Citations* treats cases reported in the *Federal Reporter, Federal*

*Supplement* and *Federal Rules Decisions.* Shepard's also provides parallel citations. Using Shepard's is essential in legal research. Hands-on use is the best experience for learning the use of *Shepard's Citations.*

## ENCYCLOPEDIAS

All the above-discussed materials are primary sources or indexes to them. Because of the voluminous nature of the primary sources and the legalese contained within them, it is often easier to begin legal research in secondary sources such as encyclopedias. Legal encyclopedias are arranged by subject and contain footnotes to cases in point. The narrative articles are generally descriptive and state legal propositions in an introductory manner. They can provide background reading on a point of law and be used to locate cases from which the encyclopedia's definitions were derived. The cited cases should be read and looked up in *Shepard's Citations* to see if they are still good authority.

There are two major legal encyclopedias. *Corpus Juris Secundum (CJS)* is published by West. The Lawyers' edition is *American Jurisprudence 2d (Am. Jur. 2d). Corpus Juris Secundum* attempts to be comprehensive in its treatment of U.S. law. It claims to cite all reported cases in its footnotes. It provides West's topic and key numbers. *American Jurisprudence 2d* cites only selected decisions and provides citations to *ALR* annotations. Thus, it can be used for quick answers, and then *ALR* can be consulted for in-depth treatment.

## DICTIONARIES AND DIRECTORIES

At least one of two legal dictionaries can be found in most libraries. They are *Ballentine's Law Dictionary with Pronunciations* and *Black's Law Dictionary.* In addition to the definitions of legal terms, Black's provides a table of abbreviations used in legal publications.

The primary directory of attorneys is the *Martindale-Hubbell Law Directory.* It is a comprehensive directory of attorneys for the entire United States. An interesting feature is the confidential ratings, which estimate legal ability, recommendations and promptness in paying bills. Local libraries will generally contain state and local directories and phone company yellow pages which list attorneys.

## PERIODICALS

Another important secondary source for legal materials is legal periodicals. Scholarly journals in law are often published by bar associations and law schools. The articles are generally written by law school students and faculty and scholars from related disciplines. They provide commentary on cases, societal issues and jurisprudence. An example of a law school review is the *Harvard Law Review.* An example of a bar association publication is the *American Bar Association Journal.*

Like other journals, law periodicals are indexed in indexing services. The *Index to Legal Periodicals* indexes articles by subject and author. It contains a table of cases commented upon, which serves as an index to case commentary in law journals, and an index to book reviews. There are also the *Current Law Index* and the *Legal Resource Index.* They contain author, title and subject indexes. The subject indexes use Library of Congress subject headings. They also contain tables of cases as well as tables of statutes. The *Current Law Index* is in print form and is issued monthly. The *Legal*

*Resource Index* is produced on microfilm and is contained in its own reader. It is also available as an online database on the Dialog system.

## RESEARCH GUIDES

This chapter is at best an introduction to legal research. Three books that provide more detail and include extensive illustrations are Cohen's *Legal Research in a Nutshell,* Jacobstein and Mersky's *Fundamentals of Legal Research,* and Price's *Effective Legal Research.*

Libraries that contain collections of law books will usually have at least one librarian trained in their use. Before attempting complex legal research consult with a trained law librarian. Law school libraries will contain the most extensive collection of law books, and their librarians often have law degrees in addition to library degrees. Collections of law books in other types of libraries will vary considerably.

## COMPUTERIZED LAW SERVICES

There are two major vendors of computerized legal databases. The West Publishing Company produces Westlaw. It contains the full text of the court cases in the West reporting system. Mead Data Central produces Lexis, also a full-text online database. Both are sophisticated legal research systems, and they are expensive, especially if one prints the full text of cases. However, a subject search can be performed and only the case citations printed. The citations can then be used to look up the cases in printed volumes.

## CASE CITATION

Legal citations refer to statutes, case law, court rules and procedures, legal periodicals, encyclopedias, etc. Although there is no universally accepted method of citation, they generally follow similar formats. A style manual useful for legal citing is Harvard's *A Uniform System of Citation.*

A legal citation usually consists of the following elements: names of parties involved, volume, series title abbreviated page, and year. If a case was published in an official reporter, the official citation is given first, followed by parallel citations, i.e., citations to unofficial sources. For example, the citation for Miranda versus Arizona looks like this:

Miranda v. Arizona 384 U.S. 436(1966), 16Led2d 694, 86 S.Ct.1602.

The first citation is to the official *Supreme Court Reports,* the second to the Lawyers' edition version and the third to West's.

## CONCLUSION

Finding out about the law is a time-consuming but rewarding experience. Once the basics have been learned, confidence is gained and subsequent research is easier. Because we are a litigious society and court decisions often have a major impact upon our lives, it is important to know how to find out about the law.

## SOURCES DISCUSSED

### Federal Court Decisions

#### *United States Supreme Court Reports*

Bureau of National Affairs. *United States Law Week.* Washington, DC: Bureau of National Affairs, 1933 to present.
*Supreme Court Bulletin.* Chicago: Commerce Clearing House, 1936 to present.
*Supreme Court Reporter.* St. Paul, Minnesota: West Publishing, 1883 to present.
United States. *United States Reports.* Washington, DC: U.S. GPO.
*United States Court Reports.* Rochester, New York: Lawyer's Co-operative Publishing; San Francisco, CA: Bancroft-Whitney, 1754 to present.

#### *Lower Federal Court Reports*

American Bar Association. *Mental and Physical Law Reporter.* Washington, DC: American Bar Association, 1984 to present.
Bureau of National Affairs. *Criminal Law Reporter.* Washington, DC: Bureau of National Affairs, 1967 to present.
Bureau of National Affairs. *EEOC Compliance Manual.* Washington, DC: Bureau of National Affairs, 1975 to present.
Bureau of National Affairs. *Fair Employment Practice Series.* Washington, DC: Bureau of National Affairs, 1937 to present.
Bureau of National Affairs. *Family Law Reporter.* Washington, DC: Bureau of National Affairs, 1974 to present.
Bureau of National Affairs. *Housing and Development Reporter.* Washington, DC: Bureau of National Affairs, 1973 to present.
*Education for the Handicapped Law Report.* Washington, DC: CRR Publishing, 1979 to present.
*Education Law Reporter.* St. Paul, Minnesota: West Publishing, 1982 to present.
*Equal Opportunity in Housing.* Chicago: Prentice-Hall, 1971 to present.
*Federal Cases.* St. Paul, Minnesota: West Publishing, 1894 to present.
*Federal Reporter.* St. Paul, Minnesota: West Publishing, 1880 to present.
*Federal Supplement.* St. Paul, Minnesota: West Publishing, 1932 to present.
National Abortion Rights Action League. *Abortion Law Reporter.* Washington, DC: National Abortion Rights Action League, 1976 to present.
National Juvenile Law Center. *Juvenile Law Newsletter.* St. Louis, Missouri: National Juvenile Law Center, 1972 to present.
*Poverty Law Reporter.* Chicago: Commerce Clearing House, 1968 to present.
*School Law Bulletin.* Boston: Quinlin Publishing, 1974 to present.
*Women's Rights Law Reporter.* Newark, New Jersey: Rutgers Law School and Women Rights Law Reporter, 1971 to present.

## State Court Decisions and the National Reporter System

*Atlantic Reporter.* St. Paul, Minnesota: West Publishing, 1886 to present.
*California Reporter.* St. Paul, Minnesota: West Publishing, 1960 to present.
*National Reporter Blue Book.* St. Paul, Minnesota: West Publishing, 1938 to present.
*New York Supplement.* St. Paul, Minnesota: West Publishing, 1888 to present.
*North Eastern Reporter.* St. Paul, Minnesota: West Publishing, 1885 to present.
*North Western Reporter.* St. Paul, Minnesota: West Publishing, 1879 to present.
*Pacific Reporter.* St. Paul, Minnesota: West Publishing, 1884 to present.
*South Eastern Reporter.* St. Paul, Minnesota: West Publishing, 1887 to present.
*South Western Reporter.* St. Paul, Minnesota: West Publishing, 1887 to present.
*Southern Reporter.* St. Paul, Minnesota: West Publishing, 1887 to present.

## Digests

*Century Digest.* St. Paul, Minnesota: West Publishing, 1901. 1658 to 1869.
*Decennial Digests.* St. Paul, Minnesota: West Publishing, 1897 to present.
*Federal Practice Digest.* St. Paul, Minnesota: West Publishing, 1960 to present.
*Modern Federal Practice Digest.* St. Paul, Minnesota: West Publishing, 1960 to present.
*United States Supreme Court Digest.* St. Paul, Minnesota: West Publishing.

## Annotated Law Reports

*American Law Reports.* Rochester, New York: Lawyer's Co-operative Publishing; San Francisco, CA: Bancroft-Whitney, 1919 to present.

## Federal Laws

*United States Code Annotated.* St. Paul, Minnesota: West Publishing, 1927 to present.
*United States Code Service.* Rochester, New York: Lawyer's Co-operative Publishing; San Francisco, CA: Bancroft-Whitney, 1972 to present.
United States. *United States Statutes at Large.* Washington, DC: U.S. GPO, 1789 to present.
United States. *United States Code.* Washington, DC: U.S. GPO, 1925 to present.
United States. Office of the Federal Register. National Archives and Records Administration. *Code of Federal Regulations.* Washington, DC: U.S. GPO, 1948 to present.

## Federal Court Rules and Procedures

*Federal Local Court Rules.* Wilmette, Illinois: Callaghan, 1964.
*Federal Rules Decisions.* St. Paul, Minnesota: West Publishing, 1941 to present.
*Federal Rules Service.* Wilmette, Illinois: Callaghan, 1939 to present.
*Shepard's Citations.* Colorado Springs, Colorado: Shepard's Citations.

## Encyclopedias

*American Jurisprudence. 2nd edition.* Rochester, New York: Lawyer's Co-operative Publishing; San Francisco, CA: Bancroft-Whitney, 1962.
*Corpus Juris Secundum.* Brooklyn, New York: American Law Book; St. Paul, Minnesota: West Publishing, 1936.

## Dictionaries and Directories

Ballentine, James Arthur. *Law Dictionary with Pronunciations.* 3rd edition. Rochester, New York: Lawyer's Co-operative Publishing, 1969.
Black, Henry Campbell. *Black's Law Dictionary.* 5th edition. St. Paul, Minnesota: West Publishing, 1979.
*Martindale-Hubbell Law Directory.* Summit, New Jersey: Martindale-Hubbell, 1986.

## Periodicals

*Current Law Index.* Menlo Park, California: Information Access, 1980 to present.
*Index to Legal Periodicals.* Bronx, New York: H. W. Wilson, 1909 to present.
*Legal Resource Index.* Menlo Park, California: Information Access, 1980 to present.

## Research Guides

Cohen, Morris L. *Legal Research in a Nutshell.* 4th edition. St. Paul, Minnesota: West Publishing, 1985.

Jacobstein, J. Myron and Roy M. Mersky. *Fundamentals of Legal Research.* 2nd edition. Mineola, New York: The Foundation Press, 1981.

Price, Miles Oscar. *Effective Legal Research.* 4th edition. Boston: Little, Brown, 1979.

## Computerized Law Services

Lexis. Dayton, Ohio: Mead Data Central.

Westlaw. St. Paul, Minnesota: West Publishing.

## Case Citation

Harvard Law Review Association. *A Uniform System of Citation.* 13th edition. Cambridge, Massachusetts: Gannett House, 1981.

# CHAPTER 10
# Historical Information

This chapter describes library sources that help researchers find historical information on social welfare, social work and related subjects. Rather than discuss texts that treat the history of social welfare and social work, this chapter focuses on secondary sources such as encyclopedias and subject guides useful for locating historical information and on a few primary sources widely available in print or on microfilm.

## SECONDARY SOURCES

Social work and social welfare have a rich and varied history, and social welfare archival collections encompass a wide variety of literature. Historical materials could consist of the papers of individuals or organizations that contributed to the development of social work and social welfare. Historical materials from state and local governments, mental institutions, philanthropic organizations, and educators and practitioners all contribute to the documentation and study of the history of social work and social welfare. Such materials are considered primary sources. Books and articles that discuss, analyze and interpret primary sources are referred to as secondary sources. Secondary sources may also be books that serve as guides to locating primary materials.

Primary sources, such as personal papers or organizational minutes and reports, are often donated to libraries and historical societies, which organize and preserve them and provide public access to the materials. The places where such public documents are kept are called archives. Libraries may also refer to them as special collections. Persons who acquire, organize, and preserve the materials are called archivists or special collections librarians.

Locating archival collections is difficult since many libraries do not maintain such collections and social welfare archival materials are scattered throughout the United States. Guides to bodies of literature are good starting points for locating archives and special collections. Notes and bibliographies in secondary sources will indicate primary sources and their locations. People are also important resources. Scholars of the history of social work and social welfare and archivists and special collections librarians can steer interested researchers to appropriate sources.

One guide to the literature is Webb's *Sources of Information in the Social Sciences,* previously mentioned in Chapter 2, "Reference Books." An entire chapter is devoted to listing and annotating history books, with particular emphasis on United States history. In addition to a survey of books that cover United States as well as other countries' history, it presents a survey of reference works, such as guides to the literature, bibliographies of bibliographies, retrospective bibliographies, dissertations, directories and biographical information, encyclopedias, dictionaries, and handbooks.

While it does not specifically focus on social work or social welfare, many of the cited works will discuss them to some extent.

Another guide to the literature is Ash and Miller's *Subject Collections: A Guide to Special Book Collections and Subject Emphasis as Reported by University, College, Public, and Special Libraries and Museums in the United States and Canada.* It is arranged by subject; within the subjects are state-by-state listings of institutions having such collections. For example, under "Social Work" one finds that the Chicago Historical Society houses an extensive manuscript collection on organizations and individuals that contributed to the history of social welfare and social work, and the Columbia University Libraries maintain a collection of materials covering the history and philosophy of social work.

Dictionaries and encyclopedias provide historical treatment of many subjects and should list primary sources that the authors used to write the articles. The *Encyclopedia of Social Work* and the *Biographical Dictionary of Social Welfare* both provide historical treatments and list primary sources. Romanofsky's *Social Service Organizations* also presents the historical development of many social service institutions and organizations.

The libraries of Columbia University have a particularly rich collection of historical materials on social work and social welfare. The social work library is called the Whitney M. Young, Jr. Memorial Library of Social Work. In conjunction with G. K. Hall, it published in 1980 a dictionary catalog of its entire collection. The catalog contains photo reproductions of 170,400 catalog cards representing over 60,000 volumes of all types of materials. It is divided into three parts: (1) a dictionary catalog using Library of Congress subject headings covering the main body of the collection, (2) an agency catalog covering a quasi-cataloged body of materials from voluntary and public social welfare organizations and institutions, and (3) a special projects catalog covering uncataloged master's essays and other special projects produced by the school's students from 1932 to 1974.

The Introduction to the catalog provides a glimpse into this important collection:

> In scope, the collection covers the broad span of literature pertinent to the field from 1795 to the present and incorporates the library holdings of The Charity Organization Society, The New York State Charities Aid, The Association for Improving the Condition of the Poor, The Russell Sage Foundation, The New York School of Philanthropy, and The New York School for Social Work.
>
> Historical works include numerous volumes of Great Britain's Poor Law Commissioners beginning with the *First Annual Report of the Poor Law Commissioners for England and Wales 1834–35 (1835);* Charles Booth's *Life and Labour of the People in London* (17 Vol., 1902–03); and the limited edition of Sidney and Beatrice Webb's *English Local Government. English Poor Law History: The Old Poor Law* [before 1834] (1927), *The Last Hundred Years* (1929). Early American documents include the annual reports, publications and conference proceedings of leading social service agencies and organizations such as the New York Association for Improving the Condition of the Poor (1845–1938), the New York Charity Organization Society (1882–1938), the Community Service Society of New York (1939– ), the National Conference of Charities and Correction (1874–1916), the National Conference on Social Work (1917–1956), and the National Conference on Social Welfare (1957– ). Publications of professional associations encompass the Council on Social Work Education (1952– ), as well as their predecessors. The collection also includes first editions and limited editions of many social work classics such as Amos Warner's *American Charities* (1894), Edward Devine's *Social Forces* (1910), and Mary Richmond's *Social Diagnosis* (1917).
>
> The collection is especially rich in publications of voluntary agencies, such as the Child Welfare League of America and the Family Service Association of America. The collection also incorporates a number of named collections including The Dorothy Hutchinson Collection on Children, The Meier Collection on Social Work, and the Brookdale Collection on Gerontology.

Reprinted by permission of G.K. Hall & Co.

Most social work libraries or libraries that contain extensive social work collections will probably have this catalog. Some of the materials listed in the catalog will be available through interlibrary loan, but many of the older and rarer materials will not. It would be necessary to travel to New York City to use the rarer materials, and it would be wise to write ahead to obtain permission.

There is another published dictionary catalog of interest to social work researchers. It is the catalog of the Department Library of the United States Department of Health, Education and Welfare (as it was then called), published in 1965 by G. K. Hall. Like the previously mentioned catalog, it consists of photo reproductions of approximately 850,000 catalog cards to over 500,000 volumes in the fields of education, social sciences and law. It also has the most complete set of the departmental and operating agencies' publications. The catalog is divided into an author/title catalog and a subject catalog. The department library is an amalgam of several smaller agency and institutional libraries.

## ABSTRACTS

In addition to the above sources there are two indexing and abstracting services that serve as a means to access the journal literature in history. *America: History and Life* and *Historical Abstracts* are the primary indexing and abstracting services for history journals. The former provides coverage of U.S. and Canadian history and culture in all periods and fields. It indexes essays in collections, some books and dissertations, and approximately 2,000 journals, including those of national, regional, state and local historical associations and societies. It also includes over 1,000 foreign language periodicals. *Historical Abstracts* includes articles and essays in collections dealing with world history since 1450, excluding North America. Both are published by ABC-Clio and are available as online databases from Dialog. Both services cover historical treatments of social welfare, social work, philanthropy, and related subjects. Many of the indexes and abstracts mentioned in the chapter on finding journal articles will also index history articles.

## PSYCHIATRY AND PSYCHOANALYSIS

A notable journal article by Mary Mylenki, a librarian, surveys libraries containing historical collections devoted to psychiatry and psychoanalysis. For example, she discusses the collections of the American Psychiatric Association, the Boston Psychoanalytic Society and Institute, the Chicago Institute for Psychoanalysis, the Professional Library of the Meninger Foundation and many others. The complete citation for the article may be found in the bibliography at the end of this chapter.

## PRIMARY SOURCES

There are three research collections of primary sources worth noting. They are available in microfilm and may be in large public or university libraries. One collection is entitled the *Jane Addams Papers, 1860–1960.* Jane Addams played a seminal role in the early social welfare movement in the U.S. There are more than 120,000 pages of documents organized into five parts: (1) Correspondence, (2) Documents, (3) Writings, (4) Hull-House Association Records, and (5) a Clippings File from the holdings of the Swarthmore College Peace Foundation featuring newspaper and periodical clippings about Addams and her career. There is a printed guide to the collection entitled *The Jane Addams Papers, 1860–1960: A Guide to the Microfilm Edition.*

Another microfilmed collection is the *Bureau of Social Hygiene Project and Research Files, 1913–1940.* The Bureau of Social Hygiene was founded in 1913 by John D. Rockefeller, Jr. for the "study, amelioration and prevention of those social conditions, crimes and diseases which adversely affect the well-being of society." The results of the Bureau's research activities are contained in this microfilm collection. It covers numerous social welfare and related topics. Reports and special studies from many early social welfare and related organizations are included, as is the correspondence between the Bureau and notable individuals from that period. This collection is also accompanied by a printed guide entitled *Guide to the Scholarly Resources Microfilm Edition of the Bureau of Social Hygiene Project and Research Files, 1913–1940.*

One final microfilmed collection worth noting is *The Minutes of the Board of Trustees of the Poor for Baltimore, 1933–1935.* These minutes disclose various stages of welfare service in one of the first colonial cities to establish an almshouse for the sick and indigent. Coverage extends from the early city-county almshouses to federally assisted local programs in the Depression.

## CONCLUSION

The serious student of social work and social welfare will be interested in the history of these subjects. Before beginning historical research it might be productive to consult with a scholar in the subject or an archivist, special collections librarian or history librarian for advice on where to begin. Such people may save the researcher a great deal of time and trouble, for they may know of available sources and collections not easily identifiable.

## SOURCES DISCUSSED

### Secondary Sources

Ash, Lee and William G. Miller, compilers. *Subject Collections.* 6th edition. New York: R. R. Bowker, 1985.

*Dictionary Catalog of the Whitney M. Young, Jr. Memorial Library of Social Work, Columbia University, New York.* Boston: G. K. Hall, 1980.

National Association of Social Workers. *Encyclopedia of Social Work.* 18th edition. Silver Spring, Maryland: National Association of Social Workers, 1986.

Romanofsky, Peter, editor. *Social Service Organizations.* Westport, Connecticut: Greenwood, 1978.

Trattner, William I., editor. *Biographical Dictionary of Social Welfare.* Westport, Connecticut: Greenwood, 1986.

United States. Department of Health, Education, and Welfare. *Author/Title Catalog* and *Subject Catalog of the Department Library.* Boston: G. K. Hall, 1973.

Webb, William H. et. al. *Sources of Information in the Social Sciences: A Guide to the Literature.* 3rd edition. Chicago: American Library Association, 1986.

### Abstracts

*America: History and Life.* Santa Barbara, California: ABC-Clio, 1954 to present.
*Historical Abstracts.* Santa Barbara, California: ABC-Clio, 1955 to present.

## Psychiatry and Psychoanalysis

Mylenki, Mary. "Historical Collections in Psychiatry and Psychoanalysis." *Library Trends* 30 (Spring 1982): 613–629.

## Primary Sources

*Bureau of Social Hygiene Project and Research Files, 1913–1940.* Microfilm edition. Wilmington, Delaware: Scholarly Resources, 1979. Includes a *Guide to the Scholarly Resources Microfilm Edition.*

*The Jane Addams Papers, 1860–1960.* Microfilm edition. Ann Arbor, Michigan: University Microfilms International. Includes a *Guide to the Microfilm Edition,* 1984.

*The Minutes of the Board of Trustees of the Poor for Baltimore, 1933–1935.* Wilmington, Delaware: Scholarly Resources.

# CHAPTER 11
# Keeping Current

This chapter describes several print and computerized sources of current awareness for books and journals. "Current awareness" is used to denote the process of being alerted to new developments and new literature in one's profession. Many people find that their education becomes outdated within a few years of leaving school. It is necessary to keep abreast of new professional developments and new ideas, theories, and research. Keeping up with professional changes and current literature can be difficult and time consuming. Many professions have developed continuing education programs. Continuing education is often required for recertification or strongly encouraged by professional associations.

One method for keeping up with new professional literature is to subscribe to journals that focus on specific disciplines or problem areas. Membership in professional associations often includes receiving one or more journals published or sponsored by the association. Journal subscription rates for individuals are usually reasonable, costing considerably less than they do for institutions. Even so, subscribing to a couple of professional journals in addition to popular magazines can be expensive.

Fortunately, there are several other methods for keeping up with new literature and recent developments within disciplines. These are described in this chapter. Many of the sources can be found in medium to large libraries, while others require subscribing to a current awareness service.

## ANNUAL REVIEWS

Annual reviews report developments during the preceding year and record current descriptive, analytical or statistical information. An annual review generally reviews central topics in a given discipline and serves as a guide to advances that have occurred on a research topic. The articles are usually written by recognized authorities. In addition to serving as an aid to keeping current in a field of study, annual reviews also generally provide extensive bibliographies and current definitions of concepts and serve as a source for identifying key people involved in a particular area of inquiry.

There is no annual review devoted specifically to social work, but there are numerous annual reviews on topics of relevance for social work practice and education. They serve as excellent introductions to fields of study for students and as a handy way to keep up with new developments in the field.

The following is a selection of annual reviews of the literature in subjects of relevance for social work practice and education. There are many other annual reviews for topics not covered here but of interest to the specialist in a narrow field. Annual reviews can be found by using a card catalog or online catalog or by consulting a guide to information sources, such as Webb or McInnis (both described in Chapter 2, "Brief Information: Reference Books").

## Aging

The *Annual Review of Gerontology and Geriatrics* presents interdisciplinary perspectives on progress in research, clinical practices, and program developments concerned with gerontology and geriatrics.

## Children

*Advances in Behavioral Pediatrics: A Research Annual* covers such topics as relating behavioral outcome to the care and management of neonates and infants, psychological issues surrounding the diagnosis and management of children with chronic disease or disability and hospitalized children, developments in the field of learning disabilities and school problems, psychosocial aspects of child and adolescent medicine, disorders of children's care in families, behavioral aspects of anticipatory guidance, and prevention of behavioral disorders. Approximately 10 chapters in each volume are arranged in three broad sections: infancy and early development, neuropsychology, and general psychosocial problems.

*Advances in Child Development and Behavior* presents recent advances in child psychology. It also notes standards in child psychology. Recent volumes covered childhood hyperactivity and psychopathology.

*Advances in Early Education and Day Care: An Annual Compilation of Theory and Research* reports original research and critical reviews, and conceptual analyses of theoretical and substantive issues concerned with the education, care and development of young children. Its intended audience is persons who work in and do research on early childhood education, child development, social work, public administration, etc.

*Annual Progress in Child Psychiatry and Clinical Development* presents two types of articles: original works and review articles of important substantive areas, such as mass media, family therapy, childhood psychosis, hyperactivity, learning disabilities, adolescence, racial issues, and parent-child interactions.

## Drug and Alcohol Use and Abuse

*Advances in Human Psychopharmacology* provides annual surveys, in eight to 10 chapters, of research on adult and child psychopharmacology. Emphasis is on topicality and clinical relevance for psychiatrists, physicians, psychologists, social workers and other mental health professionals who administer psychotropic drugs or work with patients who receive them.

*Advances in Substance Abuse* presents critical reviews of behavioral and biological research on various forms of addictive behavior disorders. Each volume, containing eight to 10 chapters, covers the abuse of alcohol, opiates, stimulants, depressants, psychedelics, and tobacco and excessive eating.

*Alcoholism Digest Annual* contains more than 1,200 summaries of reports, books and articles about alcoholism. It is organized into the following subjects: general, identification, education, research, treatment and rehabilitation, employment and economic productivity, legal and social aspects, traffic safety, support, and training programs.

Papers published in each volume of *Research Advances in Alcohol and Drug Problems* come from a variety of disciplines and areas of research. Topics are selective and come from fields "in which enough recent progress has been made to warrant a review." Some 800 studies are cited in each volume.

## Evaluation Studies

A broad range of topics reviewing evaluation research in many fields is included in each volume of *Evaluation Studies Review Annual.* Included are evaluation studies in mental and public health services, welfare and social services.

## Psychological Topics

*Advances in Psychological Assessment* presents 10 to 15 articles describing and evaluating selected new developments in assessment technology, innovative theoretical and methodological approaches to important issues in assessment, and summaries of the current status of important areas in the field. Historical surveys in psychological assessment are also included.

The *Annual Review of Behavior Therapy: Theory and Practice* reprints articles covering a broad range of topics in behavior therapy. Some topics vary from year to year; others, including assessment and evaluation, behavior therapy with children and adolescents, addictive behaviors, therapeutic strategies, case studies and clinical extensions, are consistently covered.

The *Annual Review of Psychology* presents approximately 15 articles in each volume, reviewing recent advances in various fields of psychology. Depending upon the importance of the topic, some are reviewed each year, others are reviewed less frequently. Each volume includes some 3,000 references.

The *Annual Survey of Psychoanalysis* includes chapters on such topics as history and assessment, theoretical and clinical studies, psychoanalytic education, psychoanalytic child psychiatry, psychoanalytic therapy, dream studies, and applied psychoanalysis. About 400 references appear in each volume.

*Current Psychiatric Therapies* reviews advances in diagnosis and treatment in multiple settings. Topics covered include childhood and adolescence, family and group therapy, alcoholism, community psychiatry, and institutional psychiatry. Some 400 references are included in each volume.

## Social Work

While not strictly an annual review, the *Social Welfare Forum: Official Proceedings of the National Conference on Social Welfare* comes the closest to being an annual review of social work and social welfare. Chapters are drawn from the annual conference, in which "major issues, concerns and challenges in the nation and the social welfare field" are reviewed. Topics likely to be covered include child welfare, community empowerment, the disabled, family services, financing and management of human services, income support, international social welfare, long-term care, deinstitutionalization, social work policy, and practice issues. Each chapter contains numerous references to recent literature.

## BOOKS

It is the impression of this author that there has recently been an increase in the number of books being published in social work and related topics. Particularly popular are how-to books which present therapies for and discussions of psychological disorders. There are, of course, book clubs that one can subscribe to in order to receive new books. Such clubs either send you books automatically or send notices of new titles for selection. Such notification sometimes includes summaries of the books.

Critical reviews of books are published in scholarly journals. Almost all of the journals described in Chapter 4, "Social Work and Related Journals," carry book reviews. There are also two journals that present only book reviews: *Contemporary Psychology* and *Contemporary Sociology.*

*Contemporary Psychology: A Journal of Reviews* is a monthly publication of the American Psychological Association. Each issue presents numerous one- to three-page reviews of recent books on a wide variety of psychological topics. It also includes biographical information about the author. In addition, there are brief reviews, notices about conference proceedings and reports of major research projects, previews of psychology textbooks, and readers' comments on reviews and books reviewed. Most of the materials reviewed are books, but films, tapes and other media are also covered.

*Contemporary Sociology: A Journal of Reviews* is published bimonthly by the American Sociological Association. It presents lengthy, in-depth reviews of those sociologically oriented books judged most significant. It also publishes review essays and reviews symposia. Foreign language titles are reviewed selectively, and there are occasional surveys of recent sociological literature in lesser known languages. Many of the reviews are topical, i.e., several related titles are grouped together. It covers almost 700 books a year.

For true bibliophiles there is the *Weekly Record,* published by the R. R. Bowker Company. It is a compilation of current titles recently catalogued by the Library of Congress and titles selected by Bowker's staff for inclusion. It does not include federal, state or city publications and does not present reviews. Because it is published weekly and can be found in most libraries, it is a useful current awareness tool. Reviews of books listed in the *Weekly Record* will not appear for some time in the professional literature.

## JOURNALS

Keeping up with the journal literature can be an overwhelming task. There are so many journals in social work alone that one cannot possibly scan them all for articles of interest. Many libraries will display recently received titles, but it is still necessary to look through each issue. Because of the importance of keeping up with the journal literature, especially for researchers, the Institute for Scientific Information (ISI), a private, commercial publishing company, publishes a current awareness service entitled *Current Contents.* It is divided into several separate series: Physical and Chemical Sciences; Engineering, Technology and Applied Sciences; Life Sciences: Agriculture, Biology and Environmental Sciences; Arts and Humanities; Clinical Practice; and Social and Behavioral Sciences.

The last is of interest to social workers and other human services personnel. Each weekly issue covers sociology, anthropology, linguistics, social issues and philosophy, psychology, psychiatry, public health and social medicine, rehabilitation and special education, education, library and information science, geography, planning and development, political science and history, law, economics, and business and management. Social work journals are included.

As ISI receives journals it photocopies the title pages and compiles them for *Current Contents.* It is only necessary to scan the titles to select articles to look up and read. ISI also indexes the journals it receives for inclusion in its database Social SciSearch and its print counterpart, *Social Sciences Citation Index.* There are corresponding publications for the sciences and for the arts and humanities.

In addition to the reproduced title pages, *Current Contents* has "Current Book Contents," which highlights the tables of contents for selected new publications, and a

"Press Digest," which presents direct quotations from journal and newspaper articles. The "Press Digest" section is often thematic and devoted to hot topics covered in the press and in scholarly journals. The citation for the article from which the quote was taken is provided. ISI also provides a Request-A-Print service. They will send you a copy of a requested article for a fee.

The American Psychological Association also provides a type of current awareness service to subscribers. It uses its PsycInfo database (described in Chapter 5, "Computerized Literature Searches and Databases) to produce quarterly publications on narrow aspects of psychology. The publication is entitled *PsycSCAN* and there are four volumes in the series: *Applied Psychology, Clinical Psychology, Developmental Psychology,* and *LD/MR* (learning disorders and mental retardation).

The subscriber selects the journals to be included, thus making this a customized service. This feature allows the subscriber to tailor the publication to his or her own needs. Each quarterly volume has about 75 pages; almost 1,500 citations and abstracts are presented in one year. Keep in mind that *Psychological Abstracts* is a monthly publication while the *PsycSCAN* series is quarterly.

One of the most frequently published indexing services is the *PAIS Bulletin* (described in Chapter 3, "Journal and Newspaper Articles"). Because it is issued every two weeks it can be considered a current awareness service. It is multidisciplinary and includes pamphlets, selected government publications, reports of public and private agencies and periodical articles relating to economic and social conditions, public administration, and international relations. It includes statistical studies and can be found in most libraries.

## SELECTIVE DISSEMINATION OF INFORMATION

Selective dissemination of information (SDI) is a service provided by the major computer database vendors described in Chapter 5. It consists of permanently storing a subject search strategy in the vendor's computer banks and running the search against selected databases when they are updated with new citations. The requester of the service automatically receives a printout through the mail. SDI alerts the requester to new articles and other materials on a subject of interest. The requester does not have to remember to ask for a new search every few months. For example, if you are interested in new therapies for or articles on alcoholism, you could have a search run on PsycInfo or the Alcohol Use/Abuse databases or even Medline whenever the databases are updated. SDI services vary by company, and not all databases have this feature. Prices also vary, so it is best to contact one of the database vendors and inquire about the service. Many libraries and private companies that provide computer searches can also provide SDI services.

Because new literature is so important for some disciplines, BRS provides a current awareness database called Medical and Psychological Previews. It provides access to the current literature of clinical medicine and psychology contained in almost 160 journals in medicine, psychology, and related fields. It quickly indexes the articles, and the database is updated weekly. Only the current three months of the literature is included. The citations are later placed in other databases. It is more current than PsycInfo or Medline and an SDI search can be run against it.

## CONCLUSION

Many of the services described above do cost money. The value of current information and keeping up with the literature of one's profession has to be balanced against the cost. Merely subscribing to a few journals of interest does not always suffice for current awareness. Most of the print sources and many of the computerized services are available in medium to large public and university libraries.

## SOURCES DISCUSSED

### Annual Reviews

#### *Aging*

*Annual Review of Gerontology and Geriatrics.* New York: Springer Publishing, 1979 to present.

#### *Children*

*Advances in Behavioral Pediatrics: A Research Annual.* Greenwich, Connecticut: JAI, 1979 to present.
*Advances in Child Development and Behavior.* New York: Springer Publishing, 1969 to present.
*Advances in Early Education and Day Care: An Annual Compilation of Theory and Research.* Greenwich, Connecticut: JAI, 1979 to present.
*Annual Progress in Child Psychiatry and Child Development.* New York: Brunner/Mazel, 1968 to present.

#### *Drug and Alcohol Use and Abuse*

*Advances in Human Psychopharmacology.* Greenwich, Connecticut: JAI, 1980 to present.
*Advances in Substance Abuse.* Greenwich, Connecticut: JAI, 1980 to present.
*Alcoholism Digest Annual.* Rockville, Maryland: Information Planning Associates, 1973 to present.
*Research Advances in Alcohol and Drug Problems.* New York: Wiley, 1974 to present.

#### *Evaluation Studies*

*Evaluation Studies Review Annual.* Beverly Hills, California: Sage, 1976 to present.

#### *Psychological Topics*

*Advances in Psychological Assessment.* Palo Alto, California: Science and Behavior Books, 1968 to present.
*Annual Review of Behavior Therapy: Theory and Practice.* New York: Brunner/Mazel, 1973 to present.
*Annual Review of Psychology.* Palo Alto, California: Annual Reviews, 1950 to present.
*Annual Review of the Schizophrenic Syndrome.* New York: Brunner/Mazel, 1971 to present.
*Annual Survey of Psychoanalysis.* New York: International Universities Press, 1952 to present.
*Current Psychiatric Therapies.* New York: Grune and Stratton, 1961 to present.

#### *Social Work*

*Social Welfare Forum: Official Proceedings of the National Conference on Social Welfare.* New York: Columbia University Press.

## Books

American Psychological Association. *Contemporary Psychology: A Journal of Reviews.* Washington, DC: American Psychological Association, 1956 to present.
American Psychological Association. *Contemporary Sociology: A Journal of Reviews.* Washington, DC: American Sociological Association, 1972 to present.
*Weekly Record.* New York: R. R. Bowker, 1974 to present.

## Journals

American Psychological Association. *Psychological Abstracts.* Washington, DC: American Psychological Association, 1927 to present.
American Psychological Association. *PsycSCAN: Applied Psychology.* Washington, DC: American Psychological Association. Quarterly.
American Psychological Association. *PsycSCAN: Clinical Psychology.* Washington, DC: American Psychological Association. Quarterly.
American Psychological Association. *PsycSCAN: Developmental Psychology.* Washington, DC: American Psychological Association. Quarterly.
American Psychological Association. *PsycSCAN: LD/MR.* Washington, DC: American Psychological Association. Quarterly.
Institute for Scientific Information. *Current Contents.* Philadelphia, Pennsylvania: Institute for Scientific Information, 1961 to present.
Medical and Psychological Previews. Online database. Producer: BRS. Current three months.
*Public Affairs Information Service Bulletin.* New York: PAIS, 1915 to present.

# INDEX

## Compiled by Linda Webster